RISE OF THE UNITED EMPIRE LOYALISTS (A SKETCH OF AMERICAN HISTORY)

Published @ 2017 Trieste Publishing Pty Ltd

ISBN 9780649031399

Rise of the United Empire Loyalists (A Sketch of American History) by Frederic Gregory Forsyth Fronsac

Except for use in any review, the reproduction or utilisation of this work in whole or in part in any form by any electronic, mechanical or other means, now known or hereafter invented, including xerography, photocopying and recording, or in any information storage or retrieval system, is forbidden without the permission of the publisher, Trieste Publishing Pty Ltd, PO Box 1576 Collingwood, Victoria 3066 Australia.

All rights reserved.

Edited by Trieste Publishing Pty Ltd.
Cover @ 2017

This book is sold subject to the condition that it shall not, by way of trade or otherwise, be lent, re-sold, hired out, or otherwise circulated without the publisher's prior consent in any form or binding or cover other than that in which it is published and without a similar condition including this condition being imposed on the subsequent purchaser.

www.triestepublishing.com

FREDERIC GREGORY FORSYTH FRONSAC

RISE OF THE UNITED EMPIRE LOYALISTS (A SKETCH OF AMERICAN HISTORY)

RISE OF THE

UNITED EMPIRE LOYALISTS

(A Sketch of American History)

—BY—

The VISCOUNT DE FRONSAC.

Price $1.

KINGSTON, ONT.,
BRITISH WHIG PUBLISHING COMPANY LIMITED,
1906.

Rise of the United Empire Loyalists

By the Viscount de Fronsac.

INTRODUCTION.

The United Empire Loyalists of the British Colonies in North America of all branches of the Aryan race:—French, English, Dutch, German,—whose posterity had settled in America are those who decided that as much of the empire in America as they were able to preserve in 1783 should be saved from republican revolution and democratic destruction. In the cases of many it was not affection for the British name and connection, since many were of different nationalities, but it was attachment to a constitutional and monarchial umpireship of affairs. In fact, many others, of the foremost royalists, were opposed in principle to the House of Hanover on the British throne, considering its right as resting on parliamentary usurpation rather than on the constitution. But they advanced nevertheless to sustain the principle of monarchy which it represented in opposition to the leveling, unpatriotic and unconstitutional democracy to which it was opposed.

The United Empire Loyalist position then is a dual one; first as a maintenance of the royalty and the classes represented in the ancient charters of the Anglo-American colonies, secondly as a defiance of parliamentary interference from Britain in the functions of the crown in the colonies—a recognized protest that no ministers, committee or parliament in England shall stand between the king and royal and constitutional government in the colonies.

But to understand this doctrine which is so vital to the history of Canada—on the defence of which rests the integrity of its institutions and the treaties guaranteeing them, it is necessary to go to the very beginning, to the causes of the foundation of the Anglo-American colonies and to the elements which enter therein, on which these institutions in Canada are based and defended, against the doctrine which has overthrown them in what are now the United States of North America.

PART I.

Colonist Under the Stuarts.

It was in the very beginning of these troublesome times of the Stuart reigns that kingdoms were founded beyond the sea. In 1606 King James I. granted a charter to two companies to extend his empire in America, the Company of London, whose territory extended from Old Point Comfort 200 miles northwest and 200 miles southwest, and the Company of Plymouth whose grant commenced 100 miles further north than the former company's.

The *motive* which prompted the first settler to go from England to Virginia, as the northern division was called, was for commercial self-interest; the finding of gold and the acquiring of estates. But the *motive* of the king in extending his empire beyond seas was to create regal states,—states whose autonomies might resemble in every feature the autonomy of the parent state as a mirror reflects an image.

This idea of the Stuarts was not original. Had it been original it would have been unnatural, on a false, unconstitutional basis. The Bourbons had practised it before in Canada. This idea of the Stuarts and Bourbons was borrowed from the feudal system and the feudal system had been derived from the Frankish allotment of responsibility to semi-independent princes over tracks of conquered domain, wherein each prince was sovereign within his allotment, being responsible only to the supreme majesty, the King or Emperor at the head of all the states, which these allotments of domain were forming. In a government of this sort, if the King or Emperor might be coerced by the democracy of his own particular state—as that which had murdered King Charles I.—the King or Emperor could summon the princes of these inferior states, who, true to their responsibility, holding fealty to the King, and not to the parliament, or democracy, were bound to rally their own proper warriors and crush the enemies of the empire, at the mandate of their Suzerain. This faith, this fealty, this knightly obligation, could be expected only of a knightly race—it would fail in the hands of such a civilization as that which commercialism causes to flourish —a civilization without a *class of honor.* It was this class of honor, therefore; derived in inspiration from that Frankish chivalry—"formed by the hand of God" —that each sub-chieftain, or prince, or council of feudatories who held a charter from the Stuart King to found colonies beyond seas, hastened to develop and put in command in each their colonies—to the end that their autonomies might be as royal and sovereign as that of the parent state and subservient only to the sovereign thereof.

Beginning with this method all the charters granted by the Stuarts for the establishment of colonies in America were in the sense of feudal holdings and of a royal character. This made them so different from the modifications which they received under the succeeding House of Hanover, when the charters became subservient to parliamentary jurisdiction and were modelled after the commissions of joint-stock companies for colonial management and exploitation. Under the Stuarts the system employed rendered it impossible for parliament to intermeddle in colonial affairs. The right of domain in the colony was vested by the Crown in a person, or a company to rule according to the terms of the grant from the Crown which gave him or them the control of that domain, with power to choose not only the officers and to make subinfeudations, but to name their successors, unless the grant was declared hereditary—like the principality of Maryland in the family of Lord Baltimore.

Holding from the King, as an ancient feudal vassal of the Age of Chivalry, the colonies as fiefs were made to respond, not to parliament which could not enter a fief, but to the King's great vassals, the colonial proprietors, or council of proprietors. In their own name, with sovereign power absolute over their colonial fiefs, they granted lands and dignities to be held solely by themselves. Those receiving grants and dignities in the colonies were responsible to their feudal superior, the proprietor, or council of proprietors and he or they to the King. In this manner the colonies were made royal even when England itself was becoming parliamentarian and republican. In this manner, from the subinfeudations granted by the proprietor, prince, or council of proprietors in the colonies to antrustians—to officers, gentlemen and others on whose honor the proprietor might rely for support military and administrative, a *class of honor* was being built up, a colonial aristocracy having many of the features of the ancient chivalry after whose feudal pattern and nature of fealty it was modeled.

That this was the best system may be understood by reason and history proves it by facts. It built up faith and honesty in the entire population wherever it was introduced; it developed a local centre of administration, free from parliamentary interference and in harmony with the condition requisite for local prosperity. During that period, after the first hardships of colonization had been conquered, the greatest happiness and contentment prevailed in the colonies, and the best of those ancient colonial residences, preserved to modern times, show in their design the aspiration and character of the leading families, whose colonial importance under the Stuarts is the proudest boast of their descendants of the present day.

In adopting this system the Stuarts were acting along constitutional lines. In regard to the nature of the population, the full meaning of the common law of England was put in active force. This common law recognizes the three classes into which every people is divided: I, the nobility, II, the professional class and, III, the burgesses. The charter of every Stuart colony made a provision for the just representation of each. In some colonies this representation was made more definite than in others, but in all there was a provision for it.

The charter granted to Virginia in 1606 introduced the land tenure system of England into the country. Now in that early settlement period, on account of the lack of an exalted motive on the part of the first adventurers going into the country, the only idea in their minds was, as herebefore stated, the acquisition of wealth, and finally, estate. The English law was established. According to English law, not only a city but a division of the country must be erected into a "borough" before it might be represented in the legislature. But no baronial or manorial grant was made in Virginia from the earliest date down to the extinction of Crown authority beneath the democratic American revolution. A great many "broken" gentlemen had come over even with the first colonists, and they were not of a good quality of their own class. There were a few who thought of restoring their family station "in the pomp of heraldry" and the pride of statecraft, and of erecting manours and baronies in the new world in the romantic spirit of old Europe. But the records show that these "decayed gentlemen" were in general the least valuable of all the colonists to Virginia. In fact, had it not been for the indominatable courage and genius of a soldier among them, Capt. John Smith, the early colonists would have perished from their own dissipation and ignorance and lack of cohesive energy. Smith organized the necessary labors to be performed and compelled their performance by his authority as chief of the colony, he having been appointed to that position by the "London Council" in control of the colony. This Council consisting of thirteen of the British nobility held the colony as a direct feudatory of the Crown, who were to administer the colony according to the provisions of the charter. This charter was the constitution of Virginia and as such was an abstract of the Common Law of England. In addition this abstract provided that:

I. The Christian religion, Church of England, shall be maintained and the clergy paid from certain revenues of the colony.

II. Lands are to descend as in England. The entailment of estates among the aristocracy was encouraged as a measure necessary for local prosperity and for the independence and well-being of that aristocracy.

The officers of a colony were to consist of a governor appointed by the great feudatories—the London Council,—assisted by councellors chosen in the colony from among the great land owners. Later there was added a House of Burgesses elected by the remaining inhabitants, whose office, as every representative office is, was to present their grievances to be remedied to the Governor and Council, and to vote the money necessary to carry on the government of the colony. Apart from the taxation and asssessment subject to the House of Burgesses, the Governor and Council—in the name of the great feudatories of the colony (London Council) —administered the feudal lands, known usually as "Crown lands."

The early gentlemen colonists of Virginia, who settled Jamestown on the James River in 1607, had their connection broken with their families in Britain, several leaving England to escape the consequences of their debts. On this account they were unable to obtain wives of their own class, even after they had gained appropriate estates in the colony. They knew no other class than their own in Britain. It became necessary for their domestic happiness to have wives of some kind however, and they employed an agent in London, who for the sake of 40 pounds of tobacco for each respectable female whom he could induce to go to Virginia and marry one of the planters, agreed to send over the article required for their domesticity. History does not state whether this article was a little *dear*, but it was certainly respectable, or the bargain would have been declared "off."

From the time of the settlement of Jamestown in 1607 to 1649 affairs in Britain were running more and more in a democratic channel. The people described in Cromwell's address to parliament, the leaders of this democracy, who had raised the indignation of Cromwell himself, had murdered the King, Charles I., and had usurped the royal power. All the counsellors and feudatories of the King had been killed in battle, or had fled the kingdom and some of those grand old cavaliers came to Virginia at this time, as fugitives, burning with indignation against the unprincipled and presumptuous democracy, whom they had left behind in Britain in the house of empire.

"For there was dust of vulgar feet
On that polluted floor;
And perjured traitors filled the seat
Where good men sat before."

It was at this time that the old feudal fealty showed itself in Virginia, being given an opportunity of expression in favor of the Crown of which Virginia was a fief. It was at this time that Sir William Berkeley was governor of Virginia, one of those few knightly souls of old Europe who came to America and whose renown is worthy to live forever in the pages of chivalry. "He belonged to an ancient English family; believed in monarchy as a devotee believes in his saint, and brought to the little capital at Jamestown all the graces, amenities and well-bred ways which at that time were articles of faith with the cavaliers. He was certainly a cavalier of cavaliers, taking that word to signify an adherent of *monarchy* and the Established Church. For these, this smiling gentleman was going to fight like a tiger or a ruffian. The glove was of velvet but under it was the iron hand which would fall inexorably alike on the New England Puritans and the followers of Bacon"—Cook's *"Hist. of Virginia"* p. 182.

And he was right in his severity, for force only can keep fraud at bay!

To write the life of Berkeley could be done better in verse than in prose. He was a hero—a *"Rokeby"*— the only hero in all the history of the thirteen English colonies of North America whose personality is surrounded by the halo of romance. His mind was exalted, keen and active. He wrote a *"Discourse and View of Virginia"* and his drama *"The Lost Lady"* was acted in London and made an impression for its merit and character on Pepys. He was an able administrator and looked after the prosperity of the colony in material things. He set an example to planters in the manner in which he cultivated his estate of "Greenspring" ten miles from Jamestown, where he raised 1500 apple trees, besides apricots, peaches, pears, quinces and "mellicottons." The colony under his administration advanced to a population of 40,000. In his hospitality he was unbounded. The noble generosity of his soul caused him to stand with knightly valor by those who had pledged themselves in the same cause, through the calamities of misfortune and the dangers of civil strife. "When afterwards, in the stormy times, the poor cavaliers flocked to Virginia to find a place of refuge, he entertained them in a regal fashion at 'Greenspring' "-(Cook's "*Virginia*" p. 183.)

It was at this time in 1649 that they brought the news with them—the cavalier exiles—that the monarchy was wrecked, democracy triumphant and the King murdered. It was at this time that Sir William Berkeley felt the occasion strong within him and did that act which made the memory of the whole colony of Virginia great, which gave it a reputation from his heroism and fealty that no other colony has ever achieved and which she would never had achieved without that gallant and immortal cavalier. He determined in the line of his duty, his fealty of knight to King, to rally his little power to the cause of the fallen monarchy and to cast the armed gauntlet of defiance at the mighty commonwealth of England and all her dependencies. It was his duty; and not to reason for the expediency of it, or to neglect it for the number and strength of the enemy.

According to a manuscript by a Puritan regicide in the British Museum Library, E. 665-3, pages 1604-7, on the "Surrender of the Colony of Virginia," it is related that he "laid about him very busily and very loudly all last summer both in actions and in speeches. * * * * He got the militia of the country to be of his party and nothing talked on but burning, hanging, plundering, etc., or anything rather than yield to such bloody tyrants," (as the parliament of England). What by threatening some and flattering others, the assistance of 500 Indians promised him * * * he had so far prevailed and was of late so far seconded by those unhappy gentlemen that help to ruin themselves and their King * * * * that there was indeed little else spoken of, or resolved on but ruin for this poor wicked country."

These "unhappy gentlemen" spoken of, who were brought to aid Sir William, were no doubt the few cavaliers who did come to Virginia, and the fingers of both hands are more numerous than their names. These he invited to be members of his military council, and their names are more worthy of preservation than any in the ancient history of Colonial Virginia. Then the old hero, Sir William Berkeley, thought it time to break away from all connection with such a gang of cut-throats, as he called them, and proclaim an independent monarchy in the American Colonies.

On Oct. 10, 1649, he forced the House of Burgesses to sign his proclamation, which is given in full in that very rare book "Henning's Statutes at Large of the Colony of Virginia." Vol. I. pp. 358-61.

The following is the celebrated Proclamation of an Independent Kingdom in the Colonies under Charles II., against the unconstitutional parliamentary government ruling in England:—

Act I. "Whereas divers out of ignorance, others out of malice, schism and faction, in pursuance of some design of innovation, may be presumed to prepare men's minds and inclinations to entertain a good liking of their contrivement, by casting blemishment of dishonor on the late most excellent and now undoubtedly sainted King, and to those close ends vindicating and attesting the late proceedings against the late blessed King (though by so much they may seem to have color of law and form of justice, they may be truly said to have the more and greater height of impudence); and on this foundation of asserting the clearness and legality of the said unparalleled treasons, perpetuated on the said King, do build hopes and inferences to the high dishonor of the regal state, and in truth to the utter disinheritance of His Most Sacred Majesty that now is, and the divesting of him of these rights which the law of Nature and of Nations and the known laws of the Kingdom of England have adjudged inherent to his royal line and the law of God, himself (if sacred writ may be so styled of which this age doth loudly call in question) hath consecrated unto him. And, as arguments easily and naturally deduced from the aforesaid cursed and destructive principles, with endeavor they press and persuade the powers of the commission to be void and null, and all magistracy and offices thereon depending to have lost their vigor and efficacy, by such means assuredly expecting advantages for the accomplishment of their lawless and tyraneous intentions. Be it therefore declared and enacted by the governor, council and burgesses of this Grand Assembly and the authority of the same, that what person soever, whether stranger or inhabitant of this colony, after the date of this act, by reasoning, discourse, or argument, shall go about to defend and maintain the late traitorous proceedings against the aforesaid King of most happy memory, under any notion of law or justice, such person, using reasoning, discourse or argument, or uttering any words or speeches to such purpose, and being proven by competent witnesses, shall be adjudged an accessory, post mortem to the death of the aforesaid King and shall be proceeded against for the same according to the known laws of England; or, whoever shall go about by irreverent and scandalous language to blast the memory and honor of the late most pious King, shall on conviction suffer such censure and punishment as shall be thought fit by the governor and council. And be it further enacted, that what person soever shall by words or speeches endeavor to insinate any doubt, scruple or question of or concerning the undoubted and inherent right of His Majesty that now is, to the *colony of Virginia, and these other, His Majesty's dominions and countries*, as King and supreme Governor, such words and speeches shall be adjudged high treason.

"And it is also enacted, that what person soever, by false reports and malicious rumors, shall spread abroad among the people anything *to change of government*, or to the lessening of the power and authority of the governor, or government, either in civil or ecclesiastical causes (which this Assembly hath and doth declare to be full and plenary to all intents and purposes), such persons, not only the authors of such reports and rumors but the reporters and divulgers thereof (unless it be done by way of legal information before a magistrate) shall be adjudged equally guilty, and shall suffer such punishment even to severity, as shall be thought fit, according to the nature and quality of the offence."

The names of the Grand Assembly that proclaimed King Charles II. in Virginia were:—Sir William Berkeley, Governor. For James County, Walter Chiles, Thomas Swann, William Barrett, George Reade, William Whittaker, George Dunston. For Henrico County, William Hatcher. For Charles City, Col. Edward Hill and Charles Sparrow. For Warwick County, Col.

Thomas Harwood and John Walker. For Isle of White County, George Handy and Robert Pitt. For Nansmond County, Col. George Carter and Toby Smith. For Elizabeth City, Capt. William Worlick and Joseph Robbins. For Lower Norfolk, Barth. Hoskins and Thomas Lambert. For York County, Col. Ralph Wormley and Ralph Burnham. For Northumberland County, Col. Francis Poythers and Joseph Trussell.

CHAPTER II.

Virginia's Constitutional Right Exercised of Refusing to Recognize the English Parliament's Participation in the Royal Prerogative—External Dissensions.

"No person elsewhere on the North American Continent, says Cook's Hist. of Virginia, moved to support the King." And Berkeley was alone, for he had to give energy to the smaller souls of those few who were loyal in Virginia and to guard against the treachery and conspiracy of a body of "Puritan fanatics" who had settled in the colony.

The Puritan democracy in England began to act. In 1650 a law of parliament prohibited trade with Virginia and the West Indies and a fleet of ships was sent to suppress Sir William Berkeley and his King's adherents. Two war-ships reached Virginia in March, 1652, and one of them ascended the James River and the commander, in the name of the commonwealth of England, demanded surrender of the colony. But Berkeley never thought of surrender. He summoned his friends, had cannon placed on the high places and distributed muskets to the inhabitants. But the ship's Puritan captain recognizing those of the same sort as himself among some of the House of Burgesses, had a private interview with them, in which bribes were distributed, and the House of Burgesses voted to surrender the colony over the head of Berkeley. The parliamentary commissioners were Bennett, Clayborne and Curtis. The only requirements made was an oath of allegiance to the commonwealth of England, and those who refused to take it and abandon "Kingcraft" were to be allowed a year in which to sell their property and leave the country.

The haughty Cavalier Berkeley turned his back on the upstart carls of the Virginia democracy that surged into power in the colony with Puritanism. He went to his private estate, and in company with a few brother cavaliers not only refused to take the oath, but was too strong to be driven out. One of his followers boasted that, though "they had been reduced by the power of the Usurper they had never come under his obedience." One of the first acts of the Virginian democracy under Governor Bennett in 1652 was to curtail representation of the cavaliers and abolish the name of the King as the head of state. But Virginia was too far away for the English democracy itself to meddle with much and the Virginia democrats were too suspicious of each others integrity to accomplish all the leveling they desired. During this time, there was nothing but plundering and persecuting carried on by the triumphant democracy of the Virginia colony against neighboring Catholic proprietors and Lords of the Maryland Manours, who had no protection from any source under the "righteous" government of the Puritan usurpation, whose pretext had been for "freedom of conscience and the rights of men,"—a verbal sheep's garment for a voracious wolf.

But all these troubles ended at once, when in 1660 the news came across the water that the Scottish army of Gen. Monck, tired of Puritan hypocrisy, corruption and persecution, had marched into London, had overthrown the English republic and had proclaimed Charles II. as King.

The great Cromwell, Lord Protector of England, had died in 1658. He had stayed the persecution made by the Puritan democracy in England and muzzled the democracy itself even as Napoleon was to rout the French democracy,—both leaders using the only argument which democracy respects, the sword. Cromwell had protected the cavaliers who were in hiding in different parts of the realm, had stopped the burning of witches, and the persecution of the Jews and had maintained the integrity of the three estates. Referring to the Puritan demagogues whom he despised, he exclaimed "I hate their leveling idea; there is nothing in the minds of these men but overturn, overturn!"

On the death of Cromwell, the friends of Berkeley in Virginia took up again the feudal principle which Berkeley as a cavalier had expressed, that as Virginia was a fief of the Crown, now that the Crown had been abolished in Britain, the fealty between Virginia and England was abolished also. In March, 1660, the planters assembled at Jamestown and agreed to the following resolve: "Whereas by reason of the late distraction—which God in His mercy put a sudden period to—there *being in England no resident, absolute and generally confessed power*, be it enacted and confirmed that, the supreme power of the government of this country shall be resident in the Assembly and that all writs issue in the name of the General Assembly of Virginia until such a command or commission come out of England as shall by the Assembly be adjudged lawful." The second Act declared: "That the Hon. Sir William Berkeley shall be governor and captain-general of Virginia."

In May, Charles II. was restored in England and with him the Monarchy, and in October, 1660, he sent his own commission to Sir William Berkeley appointing him governor, which, accepted as supreme by all parties, restored the fealty of Virginia to the Crown. Thus the value of the Stuart system of erecting fiefs beyond sea into royal governments dependent solely on the command upheld by an independent and localized class of Honor was made manifest in the action of Virginia, although the initiative and energy of that action belonged only to one lion-hearted and loyal man. But the restoration was superficial in Virginia, where in truth the vast majority of the inhabitants were indifferent, cavaliers few and the democrats more numerous, with the advantage of not being encumbered by honest considerations. In 1663 a number of indentured servants were induced to break into revolt with the idea of overturning the government and having a republican model. One of them betrayed his comrades, and this revolt was extinguished. Four of the leaders were hung. The Burgesses ordered that henceforward "20 guardsmen and one officer shall attend the governor," as a protection against conspirators.

Tranquility was threatened on another side by the Baptist preachers, who, inspired with fanaticism, preached a doctrine of religious compulsion, which, if practised, would have imposed a tyranny compared to which the rule of the Spanish Inquisition would have been that of enlightened liberty. The invasion of the body politic by their "new fangled conceits and heretical inventions" was not only adverse to individual liberty, to the established estates of the colony, and to the authority of the Crown, but to human happiness and prosperity. For these reasons, they were dealt with severely, and in many places forbidden to preach.

But there was another outburst of democracy threatening Crown authority, the estates and the governorship of Berkeley more seriously than the "Revolt of the Valets" and the "Preaching of the Baptists."

The Bacon Rebellion of 1676.

It seems that when Virginia surrendered to the Puritan English Republic in 1651 that a law had been enacted that Virginia should trade only with England by means of English ships manned by English sailors. Besides this, import and export duties were levied on all the commerce of Virginia.

Even this had not aroused the complaints of the Virginians under the commonwealth, possibly because the republicans in the colony had clasped hands with the republicans in the Old Country in the matter of division of the spoil. Perhaps the Virginians might not have complained of it under the succeeding monarchy had not Charles II. granted, as a fief, the territory of Virginia and Accomac to the Earl of Arlington and Lord Culpeper. This grant was to terminate in thirty-one years unless renewed. It was no more than the original grant to the Council of London had been—it disturbed no one. If the sovereign proprietors of Virginia overstepped the limits of their holding there was an appeal to the Crown unless the Three Estates of Virginia might consider a malfeasance to be an absolution of allegiance —according to feudal law.

But republican doctrine had begun to work in Virginia and the House of Burgesses (1670) sent delegates to the King to protest against the new grant. The protest was carefully attended to. The King promised to "grant them a new charter for the settlement and confirmation of all things according to their wishes." The new charter was drafted, had received the royal signature, and was about to be dispatched to the colony, when the news of the rebellion of the faithless Virginia republicans stayed the royal concession. It seems that there was one, Nathaniel Bacon, a factious and unprincipled republican, who had worked in secret a long while among the servants and lower classes of the population and the Puritan fanatics. His course of action must be noticed in order to show the characters with whom Sir William Berkeley had to deal and who triumphed finally in the American Revolution. Bacon caused himself to be elected to the Burgesses by the unconstitutional voting of servants and non-proprietors. He caused the massacre of six Indian chiefs who had come under safe conduct to a council with the whites. Under spacious pretences of reform he rebelled against the governor and the King's authority, and with his mal-contents, who seem to have been the major part of the Virginians, considered the advisability of proclaiming independence of England and the setting up of a republic. In his rebellion, while besieging Jamestown, one of his means of protection from the cannon of the enemy was putting the wives and daughters of the planters, who were defending the town, in front of his breast-works. He plundered the private residence of the governor, which was outside the town. He succeeded in stirring up the greater part of the people for universal suffrage, indiscriminate education and the introduction of republicanism.

Berkeley, who had only 30 loyal gentlemen, was driven out of Jamestown. He took shelter in Accomac, where he had the satisfaction of hanging Capt. Carver, one of Bacon's followers, who had been sent with a fleet of small vessels to capture and bring back the governor. Berkeley and his men also captured "Gen." Bland, the chief commander of Bacon, and after many vicissitudes triumphed over the rebellion. Bacon had been succeeded in command by a "rope-dancer" named Ingram but he was reduced very speedily. The manner in which Berkeley dealt with these people was summary but just. It is illustrated by the following story:—One of Bacon's officers, named Drummond, was captured; he was brought before Berkeley, who said, "Mr. Drummond, you are very welcome. I am more glad to see you than any man in Virginia. Mr. Drummond, you shall hang in half an hour." The time was extended a little. He was tried and sentenced at noon and hung at four in the afternoon.

Twenty-three of the leaders of this rebellion were hung. Charles II., the King, did not approve of these severities, but had he shown himself severe in proportion in England it is not likely that his brother James II., who succeeded on the throne, would have been driven out, in his turn, by the sons of those traitors and deserters whom Charles allowed to plot in safety during his own reign.

As for Berkeley, the clamor of the Virginians against the punishment he meted out to their political treachery caused him to be recalled by the King, and it is said that he died "broken-hearted" in England at the ingratitude of his royal master. It is certain that all the Virginia historians, afflicted with the same complaint of which Bacon suffered, condemn Berkeley as a tyrant. Cook, the best of them says: "He was devoted to monarchy, and the church * * * * In defence of one he persecuted dissent; in support of the other he waded in blood. * * * * For a quarter of a century he ruled the colony to the fullest satisfaction of the people. He was an elegant host and a cordial companion who made everyone welcome. He displayed not the least desire to invade the rights of Virginians; on the contrary he defended them on every occasion. It may be said with truth that, in all these years, he was the sincere friend of Virginia and Virginians. All his interests and affections were centred there—in his wife and his home. It was 'the most flourishing country the sun ever shone over,' he said. But one day rebellion raised its head in this beautiful land. His idol, the Divine Right, was flouted by these old friends * * * * then he was merciless to them when they were at his mercy." (Cook's *Virginia*, p. 296-7). In other words, "he protected the rights" and maintained them, and they—what did they? They invaded the Rights of the Crown, which they had promised to respect. They, the faithless, the treacherous, the unreliable! How could

Berkeley, once they had lost all consideration of honor, feel confidence in them!!

The three great innovations on the ancient, political and social conditions against which Sir William Berkeley had to contend and which are the bane of modern states at the present, were: I, Extreme Public Education, Republicanism, and II, Universal Suffrage.

I. Berkeley was opposed to extreme public education, because it tends to declass the members of the population, and in this alone to make them restless, discontented and conceited. Not only that, but to tax the provident and industrious for the benefit of the slothful and careless—who breed like rabbits—is to handicap the better portion of the people. To buy the material of all arts, science and language by enforced taxation and give it to those who do not pay for it, which material reason and fact show that only a few can use, is teaching improvidence to be wasteful of the property of others. It is to furnish to the unprincipled additional means of dishonest livelihood, for the scientific adulteration of food and clothing, for the creation of fraudulent stock companies, and for the skilful dissemination of dishonest principles of government. It is a vain endeavor to produce a republican equality by means of "education" when education itself cannot add one quality to the mind or develop a sentiment where there is not the germ of that sentiment. All the "education" of America has not been able to produce a musician, an artist and a historian, to rank with those of old Europe, where the *Class of Sentiment* has not been destroyed by "republicanism." The Inca Turpac Yupanqui declared that "Learning was intended for those only of generous blood." The clerical classes of ancient Gaul—although possessed of the art of writing, considered the *pearls* of their tradition too precious to be cast at the feet of swine, and transmitted them to the accepted and approved members of their caste by memory only. It was the same in ancient Egypt. The criminal statistics of the United States show that the worst criminals are the best "educated." The increase of crime has gone the same way, the per cent. rising with the "advantages" offered by the free "higher education" from one in ten thousand in 1850 to one in four hundred in 1890. In the Southern States, (1890) where "public education" was not so diffused, the per cent. of criminality was less than one-half that of New England where "free education" is the longest established on a "liberal" basis. In New York and Chicago, where the public school fund embraces appropriation of millions, filched from those who do not patronize the public-schools and who do not believe in them, the criminality is much higher than in foreign cities of the same size where "education" is not so extravagant. Education of the most exalted and extravagant sort can not fill a heart with lofty sentiment where no germs of sentiment exist. In proportion as education is diffused the standard of literary excellence is lowered, and the continuance of writers of classics is diminished. Because in former days when "Learning was for those of generous blood," who are the few, their demand made the standard high; at the present time, the demand of the "educated" multitude is louder and more potent with publishers than that of the ancient few, and the standard and style are lowered to comply with the demand. The race verges then on an intellectual decline, and the age is called "materialistic" but only for this reason—that the instincts of the many are gross and unsentimental and must remain so ever, and an appeal to them as to a standard results in the exclusion of everything higher and better. Besides provision for a public education shows lack of general ethical perception—the very idea of "educating one man's children with another man's money" is proof of it. It destroys the value of inherited qualities that are not perceptible by educational means, such as generosity, magnanimity and honor,—arranged in the present condition of society as handicaps to their possessors in the race of life; the class of their possessors becomes smaller with each generation.

II. *Universal Suffrage,*—In the beginning of the settlement of Virginia, before there was any real property interest in the colony, up to the year 1655 "all settlers had a voice in public affairs, first in the daily matters of the commune, or "hundreds," and after 1619 in electing Burgesses * * * * But in 1655 it was changed by men of the commonwealth "(to cut off the influence of the retainers of the Cavaliers)." In that year the Burgesses declared that none but 'housekeepers, whether freeholders, leaseholders, or otherwise tenants,' shall be 'capable to electing Burgesses.' One year afterwards (1656) the ancient usage was restored, and all 'freemen' were allowed to vote, since it was 'something hard and unagreeable to reason that any person shall pay equal taxes and yet have no vote in the elections'; but the freemen must not vote in a tumultuous manner.' Such was the record of the first commonwealth."—(Cook's "*Virginia*.")

"In 1670, the King's men restored the first act, restricting the suffrage again. The reason is stated:— The 'usual way of choosing burgesses by the votes of *all persons, who, having served their time, are freemen in this country*,' produced 'tumults at the election.' Therefore it were better to follow the English fashion and 'grant a voyce in such election only to such as by their estates, real or personal, have interest enough to tye them to the endeavor of the public good.' So, after this, none but 'freeholders and housekeepers' were to vote."

* * * * * *

"The persons who had served their time as indentured servants had 'little interest in the country'; they were making disturbances at elections * * * * This was the determinate sentiment and the law remained settled, with the exception of one year (1676) when Bacon's Assembly changed it, declaring that 'freemen should vote.' This was swept away by a general repeal of all 'Bacon's' laws' and the freehold restriction remained the law of Virginia nearly to the present time" (1870)—Cook's *Virginia*, pp. 223-4.

Simply because passengers have purchased a railway ticket and have ridden on the cars on their journey s no reason that they ought to vote with the stockolders of the railway for the choice of directors and for the management of the road. There is but one way for them and that is to become an owner in the stock—of something beyond a railway ticket. The same law of right holds good for the state; no matter what the education of the citizen may be, if he does not own stock in the state he has no ethical right to vote for the choice of government, or for the policy of rulership.

The lack of ethical consideration in the suffrage is to be expected from the ingress into public affairs of those who have received the unethically obtained public education—of those who have been instructed, not by the laudable efforts of their own family, but from the results of public robbery—whereby one man's property is assessed for the "benefit" of another man's children. Those who have been "benefited" by this species of robbery are ready to try it over again in the state—in the legislature—in the policy of government. Disloyalty results and the kingdom is overthrown by the traitors it has nourished in its bosom, who proceed to form at once a "republic" in which those who raise the greatest clamor may rule, and in which each opposing minority is subject in turn to proscription and plunder. This is the character of the men who have instituted every "republic" that has existed in any age or clime, and this is the process which their government has followed out until, dismembered by its own corruption and infamy it has been overthrown by the sword of the dictator. But affairs did not quite come to such a pass in Virginia, because there was the strong hand of royal power over all. This did not suit the Virginians, who seem to have been a very uneasy, quarrelsome people. James II., last of the Stuarts, wishes to know why they are so "disaffected and unquiet," and they are found to be no better under William of Orange, who succeeded King James as result of the "Revolution of 1688" in England. Having established Virginia and raised it to the dignity of a kingdom and filled it full of prosperous conditions, the ingratitude of the people looked on the "passing" of the Stuarts with indifference. But they were to suffer for it later, for in 1861 their own constitution and the better class were trampled into the dust by the democracy.

PART II.—CHAPTER I.

Maryland, the Carolinas and New York—The Maryland Lords of Manors.

The charter and arrangements of colonial Maryland, the Carolinas and New York, apart from a general subinfeudation to the King, peculiar to all other feudal charters, provided for the especial establishment of patrician orders.

The colony of Maryland, of great extent from beyond the Susquehanna River on the north to the Potomac river on the south and west, was a principality conceded to the family of Calvert, Lords of Baltimore. The province contains the most beautiful, healthful and most productive part of North America—the unrivalled eastern shore of the Chesapeake Bay, as well as the less noted western shore. A region it is, with easy access to the commerce of the seas, to the richness of the land, broken into creeks and inlets teeming with the oyster, the menenoes, the terrapin; abounding in fruits including the fig, the best known area for the sweet potato and the yam. Truly the province of Maryland was a terrestrial paradise in colonial days—a paradise that even the mad extravagance, corruption, oppression and malfeasance of the grim democracy of the United States has not yet succeeded in entirely suppressing—so strong are the arms and limitations of Nature!

In the beginning, when Lord Baltimore began the settlement of the colony of which he was by grant of the King sovereign lord proprietor, he decided that an aristocracy was as necessary a part of the state as a democracy and that its function should be independent—that is, not confused with the function of democracy; that its true ancient Greek meaning of "right to rule" should be exemplified. This was in 1634, after he had brought over the first settlers to the shores of the Chesapeake. However, although the Assembly refused to pass his "Bill for Baronies," he possessed sufficient authority from the King as lord proprietor to establish manors with hereditary magistracy attached thereto. This was like what in ancient English history is called creating "barons by writ" and in old France would be termed "anoblissements."

But in regard to the power of the lord proprietor to do these things:—In the first place, the statute of Quia Emptoris, which had been enacted in the reign of King Edward I., in 1290, and which decreed that in all sales or "feoffments" of land the holder should bear allegiance not to the immediate lord or grantor but to the King, was set aside in favor of Lord Baltimore by King Charles I., so that in Maryland Lord Baltimore was sole tenant of the crown and had the power of erecting manors as though he were the King himself. While allegiance to the King was preserved, oath of office was administered in the name of the proprietor and all writs ran "In the year of our dominion." Now, the lord of a manor has a right to hold court and judge all offences happening within the limits of his manor, except the crimes of murder, counterfeiting and treason. This right is hereditary so long as the manor passes in the family from father to son. If the manor is sold all rights are transferred to the purchaser. At first no one could possess a manor but a "descendant of British or Irish," but in 1683 it was decreed that manors might be held by "any person living or trading in the province properly qualified." This was similar to the manner of holding seigneuries established by the French King, Louis XIV., in Canada, in 1663. But the seigneur, as an officer, was obliged to be the military commander over his tenants, to instruct them for the defense of the country and to settle their disputes as a magistrate.

The ancient records show that in Maryland the manorial system died out, not because it was unpopular, for no complaint is mentioned by the people against it, and the benefits as founders of the province which the lords of the manors conferred on the people could not be forgotten. But what caused it to decline was the introduction of slavery. Many ignoble and unscrupulous but enterprising persons began to use slaves on their places to do the work. A manorial grant did not authorize slavery. This was in the latter part of the seventeenth century, and as time progressed the lords of manors found themselves steadily falling behind in revenue, owing to the small return which their tenants gave them. They were eclipsed in splendor of display by the ignorant, low bred, but wealthy, parvenues whose places were worked by slaves. So, one by one, yielding to the temptation and pressure of events, the lords of the manors descended from their exalted position, sold the portions occupied by tenants to those tenants and with the money purchased slaves to work the portion of the manor reserved for themselves. So the manor disappeared in the plantation.

Those who read this should not forget that the lords of the manors of Maryland were the founders and patricians of the province. Lord Baltimore recognized them as such in the writs by which he endowed them with manorial rights. He permitted that anyone finding favor in his sight as a proper person and bringing wealth and people to the province might acquire such manorial rights on the possession of at least 2,000 acres. As an example, a part of the writ creating George Talbot, a cousin of Lord Baltimore, Lord of Susquehanna Manor in Cecil County in 1680 is here in evidence: "Know that for and in consideration that our right trusty and right well-beloved cousin and counsellor, George Talbot, of Castle Rooney, of County Roscommon, in the Kingdom of Ireland, hath undertaken, at his own proper cost and charges, to transport, or cause to be transported into the province within 12 years from date thereof 640 persons of British or Irish descent here to inhabit, and we, not only having a great love, respect and esteem for our said cousin and counsellor, but willing also to give him all due and lawful encouragement in so good design of peopling and increasing the inhabitants of this our Province of Maryland, well considering how much this will conduce to the strength and defense thereof, and that he may receive some recompense for the great charge and expense he must be at, in importing so great a number of persons into this our province aforesaid." * * * * "we have thought fit to grant unto our dear cousin and counsellor all that tract or dividend of land called Susquehanna, lying in Cecil County, in our said province. * * * containing an estimate of 32,000 acres. * * * with all the prerogatives and royalties of a manor and the magistracy thereof."

These Talbots belonged to an ancient Norman family that had been settled in Ireland for generations. Of the Catholic party, they were opposed to Protestant England, and it was the religion only of James II. that recommended him to the Catholic Irish in the days when Prince William of Orange, invited to England by the Protestants, chased King James over into Ireland. The George Talbot mentioned in this as Lord of the Manor of Susquehanna was cousin of Richard Talbot, Earl of Tyrconnell, commonly known as "Dick" Talbot, who was one of the Irish generals in the service of King James II. against the Prince of Orange in 1698. It is said that Talbot, while deputy governor, stabbed a man with whom he quarreled and fled and took refuge in a cave in Cecil county, where for a long while his food was brought him by several trained falcons. Some of the Talbot loyalists settled in Nova Scotia in 1783.

Bashford Manor, on the Wicomico, was granted to Dr. Thomas Gerrard in 1650 for an annual quit rent of 15 bushels of corn. In 1678 he sold it to Governor Thomas Notley, who divided it afterwards into small holdings and sold it, the manor then becoming extinct. The name of Governor Notley has passed into many families and preserves the memory of one of the foremost founders of Maryland.

Brooke Place Manor, in St. Mary's county, in 1654 reckoned as its lord Gov. Robert Brooke, president of Lord Baltimore's council. He had in 1650 the Manor of De la Brooke, on Battle Creek, in Calvert county. He had come from England with his wife and 10 children and brought over 28 other persons—servants, retainers and colonists. He became the commander of the county. His eldest son, Baker Brooke, was confirmed as the lord of the manor. The council of Gov. Charles Calvert met at this manor-house July 19, 1662, and it was standing until about 80 years ago. This name may be found among the loyalists of Ontario.

Cross Manor, on St. Inigoes Creek, in 1639 had been erected in favor of the Hon. Thomas Cornwaleys.

The manor-house, built of English brick, is the oldest brick house in Maryland, yet standing. Captain Cornwaleys was associated with Lord Leonard Calvert and Mr. Jerome Hawley in the government of the province. The Cornwaleys, or Cornwallis family, were represented in Nova Scotia.

Evelynton Manor, in the "Baronie of St. Mary," was conceded to the Hon. George Evelyn in 1638. He was commander of Kent county in 1637. He came as agent of Clabery & Co., of London (Claibourne's partners), and he superseded that person after that person's departure for England in 1637. He was the means of bringing Kent Island under Lord Baltimore's jurisdiction. He left the colony in 1638 and returned to England, but he had a brother, Capt. Robert Evleyn, who was interested more permanently in the province. The Evelyns are among the earliest royalist names of Quebec Province.

Warburton Manor, in Prince George's county, in 1690 owned as its lord Col. William Digges, son of Governor Digges, of Virginia, whose father was Sir Dudley Digges, master of the rolls to King Charles I. He married Jane Sewall, daughter of Lady Baltimore by her former marrriage with the Hon. Henry Sewall, of London. This manor passed to William, the eldest son of Col. Digges, and to his children, one of whom, a daughter—Jane—married Col. John Fitzgerald, of Virginia. The government of the United States purchased a part of the manor, on which was erected Fort Warburton, which was blown up in 1814. The Diggeses of the Nova Scotia loyalists, some settling in Ontario, perpetuate their traditions.

Fenwick Manor, on Cat Creek, in 1651 became the fief of Cuthbert Fenwick, member of Lord Baltimore's council. In 1659 the manor house was the scene of the trial of Edward Prescott for "hanging a witch." The only witness who was summoned was Col. John Washington, great-grandfather of President George Washington. When the day arrived for the trial instead of the witness came a letter of excuse in the following phraseology: "Because then, God willing, I intend to gette my yowng sonne baptized, all the Company and Gossips being allready invited." As the witness did not appear, the prisoner was discharged. Right Rev. Edward Fenwick, the first Roman Catholic Bishop of Cincinnati, was a descendant of Cuthbert, lord of this manor, whose only brother, Ignatius Fenwick, married Sarah Taney, of the family that produced Chief Justice Roger Brooke Taney, of the United States Supreme Court. Many other descendants of the lords of Fenwick Manor are scattered about the Western Shore and in the City of Baltimore. It is likely that the Fenwick loyalists of Nova Scotia are their best representatives.

Little Bretton Manor, granted to William Bretton in 1640, passed to the Jesuit missionaries. The house was built of English brick and is yet standing. It has a commanding position, overlooking St. Clement's Bay and the Potomac River. William Bretton came over from England in 1637 and was a member of the Assembly. His wife, Mary, was daughter of Thomas Tabbs, who came over at the same time. He brought with him, besides his wife and four-year-old son, three servants. For nearly 20 years he was clerk of the Assembly. There were several of this Bretton, or Brittain, family among the officers of the loyalist corps settled at St. John, New Brunswick, having commissions from the Province of New Jersey.

Resurrection Manor, between Town and Cuckold Creeks, was the possession of the Hon. Thomas Cornwaleys in 1650, but it passed soon after into the Snowden family. In 1659 and in 1662 the privy council of the province met there. Captain Cornwaleys came to Maryland with the first expedition and brought with him five servants. He was one of the earliest commissioners of the province. Later he returned to England. The Snowdons came from Wales in 1660 and left many descendants. A leading member of this family, Randolph Snowden, was a loyalist grantee of St. John, New Brunswick.

Portland Manor, in Anne Arundel county, was the lordship of the Darnalls, whose ancestor, Col. Henry Darnell, relative of Lord Baltimore, came over 20 years before the Protestant revolution in England. Woodyard, another residence of this family, in Prince

George's county, is in existence at the present time and is said to be the most interesting family residence in Maryland. This family has many descendants residing in the state. This name is met with in Ontario.

St. Clement's Manor, consisting of St. Clement's Island and part of the adjacent mainland, in 1639 was one of the manors of Dr. Thomas Gerrard, member of the council. It is the only one of the old mansions the records of which are preserved. From 1659 to 1672 court was held there continuously. This Dr. Thomas Gerrard was a strong Catholic, but he married a Protestant lady and became involved in the intrigues of Claibourne against Lord Baltimore. For this he was attainted of treason and was forced to fly into Virginia, in which colony he settled in the County of Westmoreland, where his descendants intermarried largely and perpetuated the name. The family came originally from Lancashire, England, where it had been seated for several generations, but the name is of Germanic origin and is met with quite frequently in localities settled by Saxon and German people. Samuel Gerrard, first president of the Bank of Montreal, was probably of this family.

St. Michael's, St. Gabriel's and Trinity Manors were the dependencies of Leonard Calvert in 1639. In 1707 these manors, with the exception of the Piney Neck estate, had passed by inheritance to the children of George Parker from the line of their mother's family, who was a daughter of Gabriel Perrot. The first of the Parker family mentioned in the annals of Maryland is William Parker, who was one of a committee commissioned during the lord protectorate of Oliver Cromwell in England to have charge of the affairs of the province, the rights of the Lords Balitmore falling in abeyance during that period, as the Lords Baltimore were royalists. There were several Parker loyalists of this family settled in New Brunswick and Nova Scotia.

St. Elizabeth's Manor, yet another belonging to Hon. Thomas Cornwaleys in 1639, was on Smith's Creek, but it became the property of the Hon. William Bladen, the first "public printer" of Maryland. His son was Gov. Thomas Bladen, who married Barbara, daughter of Sir Thomas Janssen.

St. Inigoes Manor, in St. Mary's county, was owned by Mr. Thomas Copley, better known as the Jesuit priest, Father Philip Fisher. The property is yet retained by the Jesuits.

St. Joseph's Manor, near Tom Creek, on the Patuxent, has been the lordship of the Edloes and Platers. Both these families were among the early settlers. The name of Joseph Edlow, or Edloe, is preserved among the Maryland archives as the first of that family on American shores in 1634. The Platers were disloyal to the crown in 1776, one of them, George Plater, being quite notorious for this. But probably in the transfer of the manor from one family to another other considerations than that of fealty were principal.

Bohemia Manor, in Cecil county, was conceded to Augustine Herman by Lord Baltimore to reward him for making the first map of Maryland. He was of a respectable family in Bohemia, in Europe, but had settled in the Dutch possessions of New Amsterdam, now New York, where in 1651 he married Jane Varlett. He had visited England and was thought by the Dutch to be altogether too familiar and social with the English to suit their taste. So, on one occasion, when he returned to New Amsterdam, after 1672, he was arrested and imprisoned. An old account says that he was permitted to take his famous gray horse into jail with him —which must have been in a barn—and that he mounted his horse and dashed out and, though pursued closely, he escaped by swimming with his horse the Delaware, his horse dying of exhaustion on reaching the further shore. The Augustine Manor was conceded to Herman also by Lord Baltimore.

Within the manorial domain of Bohemia was the first attempt made in America by a body of men to practice the principles of socialism by the abolition of private property. One of the sons of the lord of the manor joined this body to the great grief of his father, who manifested that grief in a codicil of his will, whereby he put the disposal of his property out of the reach of his visionary son. The families of Thomson, Foreman,

Chambers and Spencer claim descent from the lords of Bohemia Manor, and were among the loyalists who left the Province of Maryland when the ancient regime was overthrown.

Great Oak Manor, in Kent county, was the lordship of Marmaduke Tilden. His ancestors had been lords of Great Tyldens, near Marden, South Kent, England. He was cousin of Sir Richard Tylden, of Milsted. The family had possessed lands in the parishes of Brenckly, Otterden, Kennington, and Tilmanstone in the reign of King Edward III., and William Tylden paid for lands in Kent, England, when the Black Prince was knighted. Sir William Tylden, of Great Tyldens, was the grandfather of Marmaduke Tilden, lord of Great Oak Manor, a direct descendant of Sir Richard Tylden, who was seneschal to Hugh de Lacy, constable of Chester, accompanied King Richard, the Lion Hearted, to the Holy Land and fought under him at the battle of Ascalon against the Sultan Saladin in the year 1190 A.D. One of the sons of Marmaduke Tilden was his heir, also a Marmaduke, and the greatest proprietor in Kent, owning 31,350 acres. He married Rebecca Wilmer and left a numerous posterity. A famous name among the loyalists of Canada.

Eastern Neck Manor, Kent county, owned the sway of Major James Ringgold, whose father, Thomas Ringgold, came to Kent in 1650 in the fortieth year of his age, bringing his two sons, James and John. Major James Ringgold married Mary, daughter of Capt. Robert Vaughan, commander of the county. Among the descendants of this family may be counted the commander of Ringgold's artillery in the war between Mexico and the United States of 1846.

Fort Kent Manor, on Kent Island, belonged to Giles Brent. The Brents were related to the Calverts, Lords of Baltimore. They consisted of the brothers Giles and Foulk, and the sisters, Margaret and Mary, who came into the province in 1638, bringing a considerable number of servants, male and female. Of their descendants Robert Brent married Anna M. Parnham, of the family of Hon. John Pole, of the Privy Council of England; James Fenwick Brent married Laura, daughter of Gen. Walter H. Overton, of Louisiana, and Gen. Joseph L. Brent married Frances R. Kenner, daughter of Duncan Kenner, of Louisiana. Of his family, also, was Hon. Robert James Brent, one time attorney general of Maryland and an oracle of the Maryland bar. Some also were more decided for the old regime, for nearly all the Maryland gentry favored the royal cause.

Doughoregan Manor was the seat of the Carrolls, the first of whom in Maryland was Charles, who landed at Annapolis sometime in the seventeenth century. To this family belong two celebrated men in the early history of the United States—Charles Carroll of Carrollten, a signer of the Declaration of Independence, and Right. Rev. John Carroll, the first vicar general of the United States, as well as the first archbishop in Maryland. The grandson of Charles Carroll of Carrollton—John Lee Carroll—was one time governor of Maryland. Two of a junior branch of this family were among the loyalists to Nova Scotia.

Stokley Manor, whose lord was Jeremiah Laton, in 1675 bequeathed it to the "first Protestant minister who might settle in Baltimore county," so great was his desire to hear the Word spoken as it had been spoken in Massachusetts, from where he had emigrated. A branch of this family were among the settlers of King's county, Nova Scotia, in 1760, after the expulsion of the Acadian French.

St. Barbary's Manor belonged to the Carvile family, the first of whom was the Hon. George Carvile, attorney general of the province. A person of great consequence in the romance of history has been made the subject of a recent novel, "Richard Carvel," and supposed to belong to this family. In the City of St. John's, New Brunswick, Canada, a mansion house called Carvell Hall, belonging to a family of that name, being likely of Loyalist origin and mayhap from the Western Shore of Maryland.

Beaver Dam, West St. Mary's and Chaptico, with 20 other unoccupied manors, belonged to Lord Baltimore's kin until the American Revolution, when, as they were Loyalists, true to the crown, their property with that of their relative, Henry Harford, the heir of Frederick Calvert, last Lord Baltimore, and other Loyalists, was confiscated. And thus perished the last of the manors, the property of those who had nourished the province into strength and maturity.

CHAPTER II.

The South—Carolina and New York.

From the beginning of Albemarle Sound to St. Mary's River and back as far in the interior as the French claim along the Mississippi were the lands of the Carolinas named for the King, Charles II. He was reigning when the province was established as a feudal fief, having several Co-Seigneurs as Lords-Proprietors. Before this, in the early part of the 17th century there had been established a French Huguenot settlement on the St. Mary's River by de Laudauniére, under the patronage of the Admiral de Coligni of France. But the colonists had been massacred by the Spanish of Florida "not as Frenchmen but as heretics"—a proceeding that was instigated by the bigot Queen of France, Catherine de Medici—the same who planned the massacre of St. Bartholomew in that country. But the Spaniards paid dear for it, for a French Huguenot Lord, Dominic de Gourgues, fitted out an expedition by the sale of his estate for the purpose, and landed with an armed force at St. Mary's, where the Spanish had built a fort. This he captured and hung every mother's son of them on crosses about the place with the words above each "Not as Spaniards but as murderers."

This was the land, now vacant, which King Charles II. granted, as a co-seigneurie to a company of the British noblesse at the head of whom was the Duke of Beaufort. The manner in which they subinfeudated the territory was into twelve counties; each county into eight seigneuries, eight baronies and twenty-four communes. The titles of Landgrave, with the rank of earl, and Cacique, with the rank of viscount, were granted to certain of the gentry who undertook to settle in the country and aid with their arms and wealth in the establishment and rulership of the colony. A landgrave received four baronies and a cacique two with seats in the local council, or high court, of the colony. Tracts of land of more than 3000 acres and less than 12000 might be erected into manours with courtsleet. The communes were divided into lots for tenants to hold of the Lords-Proprietors if they did not chose to be tenants of the Landgraves and Caciques. Every tenant, or colonist, was obliged to swear allegiance to the King and constitution of the province.

The high-court or parliament at first consisted of ten members, one-half chosen by the Lords-Proprietors and one-half by the free-holders, but later seven became the number of representatives for the Lords-Proprietors. The Landgraves were John Locke, the philosopher (1671), Sir John Yeamans (1671), James Cartaret (1670), James Colleton (1670), Sir Edmund Andros (1672, Joseph West (1674), Joseph Morton (1681), Thomas Colleton (1681), Daniel Axtell (1681), Sir Richard Kirle (1684), John Price (1686) who alienated in favor of Thomas Lowndes. There was also a gentleman named Smith among the Landgraves whose title passed to the Rhett family. One of the Bellinger family became possessed later with one of these titles. Of the early Caciques were Capt. Wilkinson (1681), Maj. Thomas Rowe (1682), John Gibbes (1682), Thomas Amy (1682), John Smith (1682), John Moncke (1683). The government of which they were the controlling factors subsisted until 1692, when the King purchased from the Lords-proprietors their sovereignty and issued a royal charter by commission to the governors. The province became divided into North and South Carolina and the Landgraves and Caciques, retaining right to their titles, honors and estates, were obliged to share the privileges of the council, or upper house, of the local government, with the other gentry of the colony, while a lower house, or assembly, was created for the representation of the free-holders in general.

The Historical Collection of South Carolina is here evidenced, Vol. I., p. 276. "From that period of which the right and title of the land of Carolina were sold and surrendered, by the Lords-proprietors, to the King, and he assumed the immediate care and government of the province, a new era commences in the annals of that country, which may be called the era of its *freedom, security and happiness*. The Carolinians who had labored long under innumerable hardships and troubles from a weak proprietary establishment, obtained at length the great object of their desires—*a royal government* the constitution of which depends on commissions issued to a governor by the crown, and the instructions which attend these commissions. The governor and royal council formed the executive judiciary and military departments and were assisted in the legislative function by an assembly elected by the free-holders, as in the other provinces." The aristocracy of South Carolina has claimed from the first a most prominent place in the history of the Anglo-American colonies by reason of its firm establishment, its high ancestry and its strong hold on the administration of affairs—a hold which was weakened by the revolution of 1776 and disappeared entirely before the close of the civil war of 1861-5—to be replaced by that of the debased and servile democracy of the modern republic.

New York.

The Dutch had the earliest establishments in New York, although all that land had been within the empire of Charles V. and the claims of the French. The territory of the Dutch Province of New Netherland was colonized by them under patronage of the Dutch West Indian Company early in the 17th century, and extended from the Connecticut River to Maryland. True to the constitutional law of Europe they represented the aristocracy not only in the administration but in territorial holdings and magistracy. In Section III. of the charter of New Netherland, Vol. I., p. 370 N.Y. Hist. Coll., Second Series, it declares: "That all such be acknowledged *Patroons* of New Netherland who shall within the space of four years next, after they have given notice to any of the chambers (or colleges) of the West Indian Company here (Amsterdam) or to the commander-in-chief there (America) undertake to plant a colony there of fifty persons to be shipped from here."

"IV. That from the time that they make known the situation of the places where they propose to settle colonies, they shall have the preference of all then to the absolute property of such lands as they have chosen."

"V. That Patroons by virtue of their power shall

and may be permitted at such places as they shall settle their colonies to extend their limits 12 miles along shore."

"VI. That they shall possess forever and enjoy all the lands lying within said limits * * * and also the chief command and lower jurisdiction * * * No person to be privileged to fish or hunt but by permit of the Patroons * * * And when one may establish one or more cities (towns) he shall have power and authority to commission officers and magistrates."

* * * * * *

"XIX. No colonist or servant shall be permitted to leave his Patroon without permission."

Among the servants and menials who were transported to the colony, was one named Vanderbilt. He was direct ancestor of the rich Vanderbilts of New York and of the present Consuelo, Duchess of Marlborough. Such rise from hovel to palace, unless assisted by real merit of race, can happen only under corrupt and republican regimes, among political and financial swindlers, confidence men and grafters. And when such people rise, merit and honor—"in the opposite scale of the balance" as Plato has said,—necessarily "must fall." This is why the relics of the ancient provincial aristocracy consider such people, in spite of their great but ill-gotten wealth, not only no better than their ancestry, but ethically much worse. How different is the aspect with which the honest and sympathizing reader regards the rise of one endowed by honest genius, struggling upward towards that place of command to which he has been prepared by Nature. From the labors of the humble cot, from the exaction of the laws of existence in other places no less lowly, he turns and nourishing the hours of his vigilance, and preparation and study by hours plucked from the sheaf of his own slumber— as the pelican feeds her offspring by drops of blood from her own bosom—he mounts the pathway to dominion. By patience, by energy, by talent, by learning, by undying loyalty to his cause, by honesty in all his obligations, by magnanimity to as honest rivals who unite finally with him for constitution and state, he succeeds

at last to the joy of the honest beholder, or perishes like
some legendary Old Guard with his face to the foe.
And that foe in politics, in finance, in sociology, is
always the political sycophant, the financial swindler
and confidence-man, the social intriguant and vandal
—all combined—who occupy that place among mankind
which the vampire, the vulture and the hyena do in the
animal creation. Amidst these two groups however
flourishing on successful chicanery and legalized fraud
may be planted the one, what king, or prince, or poten-
tate however strong and mighty is there who can expect
his empire to endure if he turn from these of honorable
achievements to those of corrupt splendor and wealth ?
These two forces are in opposition in the state, the one
the deadly enemy of the other, and as Plato says, the
one can not rise in power but the other must fall. Woe
to the state, woe to the king, if it be the fall of genius
and honor!

Among the great Dutch families of patrician degree
in New York were de Peyster, de Veber, Schuyler, Van
Brugh, Bayard, Van Ranssalaer, Stenwyck, Luyck,
Beekman, Kip, de Milt, Van Buskirk, Paurtt, Van
Curler, Colden, Cuyler, Cruger, Van Twiller, Houten,
Krieckebreck, Elkens, de Vries, Stuyvesant, Kieft.

The following manours are described in the Her-
aldic Magazine of 1867: Courtlandt, 83,000 acres, royal
patent 1697 to Stephen Van Courtlandt, descended from
the Dukes of Courland in Russia and bearing the same
blason, Argent, the wings of a wind-mill, sable, voided
of the field, between 5 etoiles gueles. His ancestor was
Stephen Van Courtlandt of South Holland in 1610,
whose son Oloff came to New York in 1649 as a free-
holder. His son, Stephen, first lord of the manour,
was mayor of New York and royal counsellor in 1677,
from whom was descended the last lord of the manor,
Col. Philip Van Courtlandt, an United Empire Loyalist in 1783.

Fordham Manour by royal patent, Nov. 13, 1671, to
John Archer, whose ancestry is traced to Humphrey
Archer, born 1527. His son John, 2nd lord of the
manour, married Sarah Odell in 1686. The best of this
family were royalists in 1776.

Manour Morrisania, by royal patent 1697 to Lewis Morris, governor of New Jersey in 1638. He descended from William Morris, gent. of Tintern, Co. Monmouth, England, and bore, 1st and 4th gules, a lion rampant, regardant or, 2nd and 3rd argent, 3 torteux in fesse; crest, a castle in flames. His son Lewis, born 1698, was a judge in admiralty as was his son Richard. The leaders of this family were U. E. L. and their property was confiscated by the republicans.

Scarsdale Manour was erected by royal patent Mar. 21, 1701, for Col. Caleb Heathcote, son of Gilbert, of Chesterfield, Co. Derby, and brother of Sir Gilbert, Lord Mayor of London. He married a daughter of Col. Smith of Long Island, former governor of Tangier. He was surveyor-general of the province. His manour passed to his daughter Ann who married James de Lancey, lieut.-governor and ancestor of that noble U. E. L. Gen. James de Lancey, of 1776-83, whose posterity are in the lower provinces.

Pelham manour, 9,166 acres, to Thomas Pell, 1666, grandson of John Pell and Margaret Overand who was son of Rev. John Pell, rector of Southwick, Co. Sussex, Eng., in 1590. His son John obtained additional patent in 1687. The family arms are: ermine, on a canton azure, a pelican or, vulned gules.

Livingston Manour, 120,000 acres, in 1686 to Robert Livingston who traced to Rev. Alex. Livingstone, of Stirling, of 1590 (Scotland). This particular family was of the extreme puritan-Presbyterian party containing several clergymen ancestors in succession.

Philipsburg Manour, 1500 square miles, royal patent of 1693 to the Royal Councillor Frederic Philippse, who was born in 1626 at Bolsward, Friesland, and whose arms were, azure a demi-lion rampant, issuing from a ducal coronet argent, crowned or; crest, the same. His son Philip married Mary, daughter of Gov. Sparks, of the Barbadoes. His son Frederic married Joanna, daughter of Gov. Anthony Rockholer, of New York, whose children were I., Col. Frederic, U.E.L., leaving 10 children; II., Philip, U.E.L.; III., Susan, married Col. Beverley Robinson, U.E.L.; IV., Mary, married Col. Morris, U.E.L.

Gardiner Manour, 3300 acres, Gardiner's Island, New York, 1639, for Col. Lionel Gardiner from England, which has been possessed by that family up to the Revolution of 1776, when its rank and privileges were destroyed.

Queen's Manour, Long Island, to the Lloyd family of illustrious Welch ancestry. Granted by royal patent in 1679. Of this family was Henry Lloyd, U.E.L., to Halifax in 1783. There has been every effort made in New York as elsewhere in those republican communities to humiliate the descendants of these families and to neglect a mention in the archives of these patrician founders of the colony.

There was always considerable hostility between the Dutch and English settlements, until it was ended by the Treaty of Breda which ceded New Netherland to England, the name of which was changed to New York, in honor of James Stuart, Duke of York, who held it as a fief from his brother, King Charles II. The article of the surrender of the province to England, stipulates "security to property, liberty of conscience and of discipline and the maintenance of existing customs of inheritance for the Dutch population" (Robert's *New York* Vol. I., p. 93). Gov. Nicholls, commissioned by the Duke of York, met 34 delegates from 17 counties Feb. 28, 1665.

Under the English administration the patroonate system of the Dutch was continued into a manorial system as in Maryland, and several manours with local magistracy established a nobility in permanent official functions. Among these manorial families may be mentioned Livingston, Morris, de Lancy, while later the Johnson obtained a baronetcy, the best of whose descendants were royalist emigres to Canada at the close of the American Revolution in 1783.

Gov. Dongan, son of an Irish baronet, succeeded Nicholls, but the extent of his authority had been diminished by the cession of New Jersey to Cartaret and another, yet he claimed for the province, Pemaquid, Martha's Vinyard and Nantucket. He had been instructed by the Duke of York to represent the nobility by a council of 10 members among whom were Stephen

Van Courtlandt and Col. Frederic Phillipse, both lords of manours. An assembly was instituted of 18 members to be elected by the freeholders of the province. The governor and council were to have authority to establish courts, appoint officers, make war and peace for the protection of the province, but the war-revenue or any excessive call could be collected only by assent of the Assembly—(Robert's *New York*, Vol. I., pp. 189-90). The Assembly had "Free liberty to consult and debate on all laws."

The first government met at Albany Oct. 17, 1683, in which was signed the following resolutions: "That the supreme authority under the King and Lord-proprietor shall reside in the governor, council and a general assembly. The elections of assembly are for all free-holders. No aid, tax, custom, loan, benevolence or imposition whatever shall be levied within this province, on any pretense, but by consent of the governor, council and representatives of the people in general assembly."

When the Duke of York became King James II. he rescinded portions of these resolutions as incompatible with the authority of the assembly and the constitution: namely, that the Lord-proprietor should not be mentioned with the King and that the general assembly was not the fount of authority in this province (which authority lies in the constitution at the head of which is the King. He extended liberty of conscience to "all persons of what religion soever," going beyond the resolution of the assembly which included only those "professing faith in God by Jesus Christ." It is worthy to observe that this King in colonies to which he had given charter (Maryland and New York) did more for liberty of conscience than all others, and above all the puritan pretentions which unseated him finally from the throne in England.

As for provincial New York, although it was the most foreign in its population of all the provinces, it furnished the most loyal example—with the exception of Georgia—of all the provinces. And Georgia, originally a part of Carolina, had been made a personal fief of Sir James Oglethorpe in 1732, and its leading people, friends of Oglethorpe and the poor-debtors to whom he had given homes in his colony, would have been unworthy the name of humanity had they been otherwise than loyal.

The Middle Colonies.

Pennsylvania had been granted by King Charles II in 1657 to William Penn, a wealthy English Quaker, whose father, Admiral Penn, had been so angry with his son for adopting "Quakerish ideas" that it aroused the son's latent obstinacy on this subject until it became a mania in him and a source of ridicule in others. He prevailed on the good nature of Charles II, however, to grant him a tract of land in America, where he might try his scheme of founding a "Quaker State."

The Quaker did not believe in war or ostentation, so all those who wished to escape the danger of the one and the expense of the other were enrolled in this peculiar sect whose members adopted a sober garb, sat with their hats on in church and in court, refused to take an oath, and "theed and thowed" all the world. It is said that they won more land in the New World by trading with the Indians on a glass-bead basis than any group of the other colonists won with the sword. They were a very prosperous and careful people. When the heirs of Penn were true to their allegiance in 1776-83 they took the occasion to cancel their obligations of debt towards them by an allegiance to the opposite party. They were never noted for hospitality on account of the cost and "ostentation."

Delaware had been in Lord Baltimore's grant as Avalon but was cut off, under the charge of Lord Deleware, for whom it was named. Its early people, some Swedes, some Dutch, some English, were like those of New Jersey, which had been separated from New York. They were the "ne'er do wells" of the neighboring colonies—a trait their descendants have preserved to the present day, so far as honest industry and liberality of spirit go. Col. Ingersoll declared in one of his books that the people of Delaware (1888) were in a state of barbarism. Among them were many of Gov. Stone's puritan colony to Maryland who had been obliged to leave Maryland on account of their factious, bigoted, and intermeddling spirit.

PART III.—CHAPTER I.

The New England Colony and Government—Founding of Plymouth and Massachusetts Bay Colonies.

It was the distinctive purpose of establishing an independent state that prompted the Massachusetts colonization. It was to set up a "commonwealth without a king and a church without a bishop" as wrote the old chronicalists. But the development of Nature will have course, in spite of men's minds to the contrary and their adverse enactments. As Momsen discovered of this law among the ancients, that even in democracy "It has at its core a monarchical principle in which the idea of a periclean commonwealth floats ever before the minds of its best citizens."

Now the reason for the attempt to set up a community "without a king and without a bishop" is traced to the preceding religious controversy in England. The king was included with the bishop, solely because the king for the time became a religious partizan and countenanced the bigotry of church ordinances. The ruler of a state must be superior to creeds and churches.

It was in 1604 when England began to turn bigot. The Bishop of London in that year procured the ratification of a "Book of Canons" of 141 articles, non-conformation to which was punishable with outlawry, excommunication and imprisonment.

At this time, Holland was more liberal than England; so a congregation of people from Gainsborough in Lincolnshire, and Scrooby in Nottinghamshire, under leadership of Rev. Richard Clifton, Prof. John Robinson and William Brewster, Esq., after many risks and persecutions, succeeded in escaping to Leyden, in Holland, in the year 1608. Here it may be added that the rigors of the doctrine of these "puritan" people were if anything severer than the papal and semi-papal from which they fled; for those who did not believe were no less heretics than they themselves were to the Church of Rome.

These Puritans who escaped from the persecution of the Church of England differed only in the elective principle of the office of the church which they adopted. They proscribed the grand music of the masters and reprobated the aesthetic ornamentation and development of life as superfluous. They rejected symbolism as a specie of idolatry. They proscribed in witchcraft and burned witches with the same fury and abhorence as the Catholics burned heretics. They gave the individual the privilege of self-representation before God and repudiated the demands of the confessional. During their residence in Holland, they enjoyed the esteem of the Dutch magistrates by their orderly conduct and attention to industry, many among them laboring as spinners and craftsmen. Yet although enjoying "complete freedom of conscience" in Holland, they reverted often to their original plan of "founding a state without a king, and a church without a bishop." Thus urged by the stimulus of this ambition, they resolved to go to America. Learning of their intent, the Dutch government offered them lands in their American possessions, but they refused, preferring an independent state.

Now as all the land in America was holden by European powers, they were obliged to obtain a charter for colonization from some one of them. They chose England, because England was their home, the provisions of an English charter would be as liberal as any and they were better acquainted with English institutions and law than with those of other states. By the provisions of this charter, which they obtained, they were obliged to take oath of allegiance to the sovereign, making the king, at least in name, the chief authority of their proposed state, being thankful to be well rid of the bishop.

In the cabin of their little ship, the "Mayflower," they outlined the measure of their own government, thus:—"November 11th, 1620, this day before we come to harbor . . . it was thought good that there should be an association and agreement, that we should combine together in one body and submit to such government and governors as we shall by common consent agree to choose." (Palfrey, Hist. of New Eng., Vol. I., p. 227.)

In 1627, Isaac de Rasiere, a prominent officer and

merchant of New Netherland (New York) wrote a description of the condition in New England:—"The governor has his council, which is chosen every year by election by the entire community, or by prolongation of term. In the inheritance they place all the children in one degree, only the eldest son has an acknowledgement for his seniority."

Soon after the news of their establishment was arrived in England, there came out a great multitude to keep company with their primitive state, among whom were some liberals and others more conventional. This new company obtained an extensive grant of land from the Crown, which grant was denominated "Massachusetts Bay." This was obtained by Sir John Rowell, kt., Sir John˙ Young, kt., Thomas Southcote, John Humphrey, John Endicott, and Simon Whitcomb, gentlemen; but there were with them a great many preachers, and the religious, or church, idea was the dominant one. May 18th, 1631, the General Court at Boston declared:— "To the end the body of the commons be preserved of honest and good men, ordered and agreed, that, for the time to come no man shall be admitted to the freedom of this body politic but such as be members of some of the churches within the same (Palfrey, I., p. 345)." That is, no member of the Church of England, no Catholic, no Quaker, no free-thinker could be a citizen of the new commonwealth. Moreover, a little later, such people when found coming to the colony, were banished with penalties against their returning. This induced a struggle of the non-bigoted.

The beginning of the fling of defiance against this theological tyranny was made by men of rank, birth and education. These demanded the magistracy. There was a provision that "the magistrates should be men of quality." After this there were three classes, mutually opposed:—1, the magistrates; 2, the clergy; 3, the citizen-electors. The magistrates, originally appointed in England, were confined thenceforward to men of rank in the colony. (Palfrey, I., p. 384.)

In 1637, by desire of this genealogical element of rank, since property was evenly divided among the children and was not a factor in the reckoning, it was decided:—"That the General Court be holden in May next (1637) for the election of magistrates, and so from time to time as occasion shall require, shall elect a certain number of magistrates for the term of their lives, as a standing council, not to be removed but on due conviction of crime," etc. The governor was president of this council. Winthrop, Endicott and Dudley were the first life-counsellors. (Palfrey I., p. 441.) About this time others were admitted to vote for the choice of military officers who were not of the congregational church, provided they were in some of the colonial military organizations. Thus early a distinction began to grow up among military men, proclaiming them to be of a different mind from those of the civil community. Before this, in 1634, under the governorship of John Endicott, who was thus false to his oath of allegiance, the red cross was cut out of the white flag of England in the colony and the pine tree was substituted as the ensign of New England. A short time after this, a ship of the king sailed into port. There was no Royal Ensign at the fort to salute. A sailor having declared the inhabitants to be rebels and traitors was imprisoned by order of the governor. The captain of the ship demanded an English flag to salute. Not one could be found in the colony. The captain agreed to loan one for temporary use at the fort. The governor's council permitted it, without taking formal action to restore the colors, after the loan had been returned—so far had they embarked with their idea of an independent state.

No sooner was the colony in a prosperous condition than colonists, some Presbyterian, some Huguenot, the former from the British Isles, the latter from France and Holland, came, attracted by this condition. With them came gradually the infiltration of loftier standards and nobler thoughts, borne from the aristocratic principality of La Rochelle that had withstood the assaults of the Catholic power in France and had made a treaty with the Protestant monarchy of England under Queen Elizabeth; that had already plotted with the great Coligny to erect the structure of a Roman commonwealth on the Carolinian shore, after the pattern of the palatine burghs of the south of Europe.

Now this idea of a Roman commonwealth, or empire, in America, borne across the sea from the south of France, legitimated in continuing the empire in America first instituted by Charles V. in the 16th century, although blotted out by Catholic intrigue, had much to do in shaping after-politics in America.

The palatine burghs of the Roman Empire in France had been Marseilles, Narbonne, Toulouse and Bessières. Those regions of France in which they were most dominant were Aquitaine and Provence. It was in the palatine burghs of these provinces that freedom of thought ventured first in Europe, in the 12th and 13th centuries, to stand erect in the glorious magnificence of its genius. In the crucible of its liberality it united the philosophy of Plato and Aristotle, which the Arabian doctors brought across the Pyrenees from the Moorish Kingdoms of Granada and Cordova, then in effulgent growth in the Spanish Peninsula. With them was carried the precepts of Mehomet to be united with those of Christ, producing a species of deism whose liberality was above all creeds. This preserved carefully all the ornate surroundings of the ancient cult; addressed in artistic verse of high-flown poetry the myths of the Ancient World and adored Art and Knowledge as the visible manifestations of Divine Genius. This rennaissance in the South of France was the brightest and most splendid of Europe. From the warm glow of its light and life, it cast a flash that fell as a menace on the dark and gloomy church of the popes. The sound of its joys of Earth's blessing awakened the wrath of the Catholic heirarchy that was striving to repress the same to its own behests. The sight of the prosperity of the teeming cities of Narbonne, Bessières and Toulouse, rich with the products of the most intelligent and best trained industry of Europe, aroused the cupidity and envy of the Catholic Christians and gave a stimulus to the Pope to pronounce an anathema against this and to preach that Albegensian Crusade which brought the savage allies of the Papacy from every country in Europe in a flood of hatred, lust and extermination. That civilization was swept away. The King of Aragon, who was of this proscription, was slain in battle, helping bravely his friends of France. The scattered remnants fled into the Pyrennian mountains, from whose dark and broken recesses marched again their descendants under their Henry of Navarre. This was the origin and the end for a time, of freedom of thought in Europe —modeled after that which had existed in the old empire of the Romans, when the dilligence of philosophers conspired to confound superstition by bringing the various gods of the world together in one temple. With a liberty like this, there can be no equality. As Lord Rosebery of the time of Beaconsfield said before the Conservative Club: "Liberty and equality are mutually exclusive." There must be room for Genius, for those who are great, else there is no liberty for them who are the gems of the human race. The rest of the world profits by it, for by the few are made all the advancements which benefit the race, and to the few is due something beyond the mockery of thanks—that is, the reins of Power and the Honor of Dominion.

This recognized truth, brought to the cities of the Roman Empire the conference of rank for merit, which should not be confounded with the feudal tenure of the Middle Ages, when the holding of a lordship was reserved for nobility of race alone. Nobility, with the Romans, went genealogically within the "gnome" (name), "gens" (race), "pater," "patricius" (father). In the degenerate application in some countries of Europe, nobility went often, but not always, with the possession of the fief, "No land, no noble." The qualities originally of race then inherred in the tenure. In the organization of each city of the Roman Empire, the senate contained the patricians, or chiefs of the nobility; the second chamber, the representatives of the trades. The duties of the senate pertained to diplomacy and military affairs; of the second chamber, to decide disputes between trades-associations; of both, to regulate taxation and expenditure. Thus all classes were represented in each city, or state, of the Roman Empire. It was the coming of people with memories of these things into the American colonies that worked a ferment and reaction against the puritan bigotry of the primitive Yankees. Therefrom, in the North, the clergy, finding a growing difference of opinion, religious and political, proceeded to stir up the most ignorant, the more numerous and intolerant of their congregations to the sending of deputies to the General Court to make stringent religious laws. Thus originated the celebrated "Blue Laws" of New England. "Forbidden to kiss wife and child on the Sabbath" was not the least of their ridiculous and contemptible ordinances. While in power, they pressed heavily on the necks of the people and imposed a tyranny of greater bigotry and oppression than even that of the Inquisition of Rome. This body, the clergy, in every state, in every clime and of every creed, has been the greatest hindrance to the friendly intercourse of peoples of different faiths. They formulated against the armorials and rank of the gentry, against the science and art of the professions, against the estates of the proprietors—unless goodly portions were devoted to their own maintenance. They are the direct cause for the sterility of artistic and chivalrous impulses in New England life, by their influence in the body politic; for the dearth of romantic elements in the communities over which they were the presiding ogres. At that time, just previous to 1639, one of them named Wheelwright received a reprimand from the magistrates and was adjudged guilty of sedition by the excessive violence of his preaching—especially at this time, when the magistrates were doing all in their power to heal the breaches among different classes caused by the clergy.

Nov. 5th, 1639, "Divers gentlemen and others, out of their care for the public weal and safety, and for the advancement of the military art and exercise of arms, desired license of the court to join themselves in one company and to have liberty to exercise themselves at such times and places as their occasions would permit." (Palfrey, I., p. 550.) It was only in such military formations that safety could be had against the wrath of the clergy. Thus was founded the Ancient and Honorable Artillery Company of Massachusetts. But at the time of its formation in 1638, the civil council, under influence of the clergy, prophesied its "ungodly" influence—that is the protection of individuals joining it against their wrath—"considering from the example of the Pratorian Band among the Romans, and the Templars in Europe, how dangerous it might be to erect a standing authority of military men, which might easily, in time, overthrow the civil power." (Winthrop, I., p. 253.)

Thus the military idea began to show itself as a means of liberating people of the better classes from the theological and levelling democracy. During this time, the spirit of an independent state was developing. In 1642, the four New England colonies assumed some of the prerogatives of sovereignty, with the king as the knot of their union, in a "firm and perpetual league of friendship and amity for offence and defence." Massachusetts went further yet and established a mint in 1652 and proceeded to coin her own money. However, this was during the protectorate of Cromwell over England and her dependencies. Cromwell favored Massachussets and promoted the military spirit in the colony. He had relied on the same weapon in England to relieve himself from the narrowness and bigotry of the theological democracy in England. With the hypocrisy usual to members of that body, they had installed themselves as the supreme power of the English parliament and were proceeding to use the government for their own purposes and to shape its destinies to conform to their belief, when Cromwell appeared before them suddenly on the day of their most iniquitous proceedings. He accused them of corruption, hypocrisy and double-dealing and caused his soldiers to drive them from the seat of authority. "There is nothing in their minds but overturn, overturn," said he.

Now the people in power in New England were mostly of the stamp of Praise God Bairbones Parliament in England, and the religious persecution went on unrestricted. Later, after Cromwell's government had passed away and Charles II. in 1660 had ascended the throne, the budget of complaints against the theological democracy of Massachussets for persecution, bloodshed, torture, banishment and loss of property and life was very large. The king sent commissioners to the colony in 1666 to report on these abuses of power. Commissioner Randolph declared that the better portion of the people had been driven away and that the public offices had fallen in the hands of the most virulent. Among others reported to the king as an abuse was the exercise of the sovereign prerogative of coining money; for although the king had been proclaimed in the colony in 1661, the pine-tree shilling was coined the very next year without any other legend than that of the sovereignty of the colony. But the king was mollified considerably when Governor John Leverett, who had been summoned to England to answer for the colony, remarked that the figure on the coin was that of the Royal Oak, which had sheltered His Majesty after the Battle of Worcester—a witty reply which gained for the Massachussetts governor the honor of knighthood.

While making the greatest professions of loyalty and agreeing that all the requirements of their charter had been fulfilled, the investigation showed that Puritan loyalty was a lie and that they had not fulfilled one of the requirements which they had promised to fulfil. The king found it necessary therefore that a new charter be given so as to bring the officers in direct contact with His Majesty's government, and that the governors be sent from England, so that they should not belong to any cabal in the colony. The Puritans had not proved themselves to be a trustworthy people. Their word could not be relied on.

CHAPTER II.

New England Colony and Government—Beginning of the Royalists in New England—The King's Chapel —The Royal Charter Re-affirmed.

As an example of the prosecution of the leveling Puritan democracy of New England whose unethical and republican ideas were being put constantly in force against all comers who were different from them, the history of the early king's Chapel of Boston is an enlightenment to those who are capable of profiting by a lesson. Besides, King's Chapel, although having passed into the hands of the enemy, is the cradle of the U. E. Loyalists from Boston and vicinity.

William Vassell had come over in 1630. He was so disgusted with Winthrop and others in authority who were ignoring their pledges to the crown, that he returned to England, but came back again to the colony determined to make a stand for freedom of conscience and liberty of the individual. He commenced by sending in the following "Remonstrance and Humble Petition" to the General Court. This was signed by five others, among them being Samuel Maverick and Robert Child. "That they could not discern in this colony a settled form of government according to the laws of England, that many thousands in these plantations of the English nation were debarred all civil employments . . . and that numerous members of the Church of England . . . were detained from the seats of the covenant of free grace." They demanded relief from these disabilities and threatened if not relieved to appeal to the High Court of England. The General Court of Massachussetts, after a great delay, rejected their petition with coarse jocoseness. "And these are the champions," said the court, "who must represent the body of non-freemen. If this be their head sure they have an unsavory head, not to be seasoned by much salt." The petitioners were fined and their papers seized.

When King Charles II. had come to the throne, the absolute rulership of this Puritan hypocrisy and chicanery was brought to an end. Bradstreet and Norton, June 28, 1662, received a letter from the king. It declared, that, "Since the principal end of that charter was, and is, the freedom of liberty of conscience, we do hereby charge and require you that freedom and liberty be duly admitted and allowed." The General Court demurred, pursed up its lips and attempted to play hide and seek with the meaning of words, to hood-wink, in fact, to come a "Yankee trick" over the commissioners sent from England. But Commissioner Randolph, an old cavalier and royalist, did not fail to see through this chicanery. He wrote back to the king, that by the means employed by the leaders of the puritan democracy, the best people had been driven out of the colony or into retirement, that menials and servants with pretentious mannerisms were in the high places. So the king thought he would abridge it all, because his own church, his own laws could not exist in his own colony on account of these people.

The English king is head of the Anglican Church, and his own church could not exist in the colony under a government elected by the Puritans, although they had promised to respect the king's authority, the Church of England and the laws of the realm. In order that the king's chapel could be built, then, it was necessary to give Massachussetts a royal charter, in which the power of appointing the chief officers should reside in the crown. On Feb. 22, this charter was made. May 15, 1686, there entered Boston harbor the "Rose," frigate, bearing a commission from the king to Joseph Dudley to act in the Royal name as president of Massachussetts, Maine, Nova Scotia and the lands between. And with her came Rev. Robert Radcliffe, first minister of the king's chapel.

In October, 1688, the foundation of king's chapel was laid on Tremont Street, in Boston, on the corner of what is now School Street. About that church gathered those far-seeing and high-minded royalists in the colony who beheld in the king's authority the only barrier against the narrow Puritan democracy, that, when in power with brute force, and, when not in power, with cunning and chicanery, sought to accomplish its purpose and impose its tyranny. As Voltaire says, it is "better to be under the paw of the lion than be knawed by a million rats."

The building of His Majesty's chapel brought the royal charter to supercede the original permit of government, which had left the power in the hands of the majority to persecute those who did not believe as they. Even the land on which the chapel stands the king's governor was obliged to appropriate as the local authorities refused to sell, and the records show that he paid the original owners four-fold the value of the land.

But the time of the Puritan triumph was coming, again, and in it they were to show "what manner of men they were." When the House of Stuart that had created the church and charter ceased to reign in England in the person of King James II., who was succeeded by William of Orange, whom the treachery and Revolution of 1688 put on the throne, the Puritan mob in Boston, according to a pamphlet printed in London in 1690, entitled "New England's Faction Discovered," proceeded to their work. They seized the governor and principal members of the king's chapel and put them in prison. "The church, itself, had great difficulty to withstand their fury, receiving the marks of their indignation and scorn by having the windows broken and the doors and walls daubed and defiled with dung and other filth in the rudest and basest manner imaginable, and the minister for his safety was forced to leave the country and go to England." But the Revolution in England, of 1688, did not go so far as the Puritan democracy of Massachusetts had hoped. Sullenly but cringingly they retraced their steps when King William of Orange showed that liberality which intelligent men hope ever to find in a king. He continued the royal favor to King's chapel and presented the service with new silver. "It was the only building in New England where the forms of the court church might be witnessed. The prayers and anthems which sounded forth in the cathedrals of the mother-country were here no longer dumb. The equipages and uniforms which made gay the little court of Boston brightened its portals.

Within, the escutcheons of the royal governors hung against the pillars." At Christmas time it was the only church that was wreathed in green, or celebrated the nativity of Christ with gladness and song of rejoicing,— for Christmas had been forbidden to be celebrated among the Puritans, because they said it was popish and idolatrous." (Hist. of King's Chapel, Vol. I.)

The sound of the first organ in New England was in King's chapel and heralded the introduction of an art, the most gracious and lovable of all arts—an art which had been forbidden to enter the Puritan democracy.

Here on the walls of the chapel were emblazoned in all the pomp of heraldry the Royal Arms, the arms of the royal governors, Dudley, Shute, Burnet, Belcher, Shirley, Andros, and those of Col. Nicholson and Capt. Hamilton. And what rays of chivalry had penetrated the thick and somber atmosphere of Puritan bigotry and intolerance were focused into a brighter light in the immediate circle of those royalists who gathered within its walls.

Sir William Shirley had done the most to prop the royal cause in the colony, and, as a means to that end, had favored the King's chapel with all his influence. In 1741, just before he was appointed governor, Lieut.-Gov. Dunbar wrote, from New Hampshire to the Board of Trade: "New England might be made a very useful colony . . . were the Church of England encouraged, it would bring them (the people) to better principles than they are now of, being generally republicans." Another cause of trouble to the Puritan republicans was the culture of art and music, which the liberties of the new charter allowed to be encouraged with the building of King's chapel. One very beautiful picture was Benjamin West's "Last Supper," which was one of the adornments of the chapel's interior. At the time of the American Revolution, when the hand of lawless violence was unrestrained against everything that had provoked republican bigotry and hate, Mr. Davis, who had the guardianship of the picture, committed it to the protection of the republican leader, John Hancock, which protectorate seems to have terminated in proprietorship, without compensation to the original owners. Now it must not be thought that all the royalists in New England were Church of

England men, or, that all in Boston were members of King's chapel. Many of the Presbyterians who came to New Hampshire, New York and Virginia, especially those from Ireland, among whose members were descendants of the Huguenots, who had followed the banner of the Marquis de Rouvigni into England and Ireland in 1688-90, were distinctly royalist, although not ardent for the domination of England. Guizot notices the royalism of the Presbyterians in his "Vie de Charles I." In Britain, after the Church of England and the monarchy had been overthrown by Cromwell and the Puritans, it was the Presbyterians who pronounced against republicanism and took up arms for the king, and finally, with Gen. Monck at their head, proclaimed Charles II. as king and entered London with their armed hosts to restore the monarchy. But among the royalists of King's chapel alone at this time, immediately preceding the republican revolution of 1776, were Peter Faneuil, who gave Faneuil Hall to the city, Dr. Gardiner, who supplied the colonial troops with medicines free of charge, and Isaac Royall who founded the first law professorship at Harvard University. Whatever was great and excellent and unselfish belonged to them. They were, in truth, as Leckey, the historian, says, "The gentry of the colonies." The entire membership of King's chapel were royalist to the core, loyal to the head of this colony, which head was the king, the emperor of all the provinces.

A month after the royal authority had left Boston, in 1776, with the British troops and the members of King's chapel, the chapel was reopened by the enemy, by the Puritan congregational republicans, whose sires had opposed the erection of the church, and had "besmeared its walls with dung" during the disturbance of 1688. They came from the Old South meeting-house, and occupied the king's property without warrant; for the king's property passed to the commonwealth by act of the Treaty of 1783, as the property of absentee royalists had passed before by the confiscation acts of 1778-9. In consequence of persecutions like the above, the democracy of Massachusetts Bay was deprived of its usurpation by order of King Charles II.

The colony of Plymouth was united to that of Massachusetts Bay, under a Royal Charter from King Charles II., Feb. 22, 1669, with the following provisions:

I. "That all householders, inhabiting in the colony, take the oath of allegiance, etc."

II. "That all men of competent estate; that is men who own property enough to enable them to have a right to vote, and civil conversation, though of different judgments, may be admitted to be freemen, and have liberty to choose and be chosen as officers both civil and military."

III. "That all men and women of orthodox opinion, competent knowledge and civil lives (not scandalous) be admitted to the sacrament of the Lord's supper, and their children to baptism, if they desire it."

IV. "That all laws and expressions of law derogatory to His Majesty, if any such have been made in these troublous times, he repealed, altered, and taken off from the file."

The Plymouth colony had fulfilled all these provisions. The Massachusetts colony had violated every one. Yet the governor and chief men of the colony testified that all had been carried out. In the first instance the oath of allegiance was not administered in Massachusetts at this time or before. In the second instance only those were allowed to vote who belonged to the Congregational church of the colony, and all others were persecuted. In the third instance no one but of the Congregational church was permitted to receive the sacraments or baptism. Laws were made forbidding any other form of worship. It was made an act of treason to appeal from the laws of the colony to the crown that had given the colony its charter. This was also a violation of the fourth requirement, because such laws were contrary to the charter from the crown on which the government of the colony existed.

Thus from the very beginning, the religious democracy of Massachusetts manifested a desire to be as far away from the royal government in everything as possible.

Roger Williams, a clergyman, desirous of religious and political liberty, fled away from the tyranny of the

Massachusetts democracy and founded the Providence Plantation in 1636, now known as Rhode Island. The Connecticut colony was established about the same time at Hartford and New Haven.

Capt. John Mason obtained a grant of land between the colony of Massachusetts and the Province of Maine, which latter was conferred on Sir Ferdinand Gorges. Mason's land was known as New Hampshire and was a royal colony. Maine was under the proprietorship of Gorges, until 1690, when it was ceded to Massachusetts.

Massachusetts then may be seen to have been not only the leading colony of the north, but the parent of three others. Indeed, her population flowed over into them all.

Plymouth and the Province of Maine were incorporated with Massachusetts in 1690. Before this the governors had been elected by the people, after 1690 they were appointed by the Crown, together with the Lieutenant-Governor and Secretary of the Province and the councillors. The governor, under the last charter, appointed also, the Judges, Sheriffs, Marshals, Provosts and military officers. The people of the colony elected their deputies to the General Court as formerly, and any man was qualified to vote and serve in any office, if elected or appointed, if he possessed land in the province to the value of 40 shillings per annum or to the worth of £50 sterling.

It was impossible after 1690 for the Puritan malignants of the colony to burn witches, persecute Quakers, drive off Episcopalians and disfranchise those who differed from them in opinions political and religious, as they had done before because the chief magistrate was now appointed by the Crown.

PART IV.—CHAPTER I.

Union Era—Parliament Usurps Crown Functions in the Provinces.

Since the Revolution of 1688, in England, during which parliament usurped all the functions of the crown, set aside the rightful dynasty and invited to the throne William of Orange, its pretentions knew no bounds; the constitution was not regarded—since had it been, the acts of parliament would have been null. The leader of this movement against the trust imposed in them by the late King James II. were a set of the most dispicable scoundrels that had ever attempted a government by revolutionary means and for the sole purpose of the booty of office. Chief of these was Marlborough the deserter, so well described by Macaulay (Hist. of England.) The set of people who flocked about them as followers were of the same quality, but of a minor degree of rascality—like those in most so-called "Liberal" parties.

Green's *"Hist. of the English People,"* Vol. IV., p. 1523, relates: "Parliament became corrupt, jealous of power, fickle in its resolves and factious in spirit. . . It grumbled at the ill-success of the war, at the suffering of the merchants, at the discontent of the churchmen, and it blamed the crown and its ministers for all at which it grumbled. . . Its mood changed, as William bitterly complained with every hour." It seems that before this date, in 1672, the late king, James II., had formed a cabinet of five members, chosen by himself, as advisers on different functions of the administration. Parliament had no right to expect a share in these functions of the crown at that time. But after the Revolution of 1688—after it had put on the throne a king of its own, it felt that it ought to be the guardian of that king, by shaping the administration through a cabinet indicated by itself. William of Orange had continued the practice of forming his cabinet without consulting parliament, and what parliament was aiming to do was to control the king's choice. But not one of its members knew how to accomplish it, as it had never been done before. The credit of solving the difficulty, of further betraying his country and bringing disaster on it in the subsequent loss of the American empire, belongs to Robert Spencer, Earl of Sunderland. He had been a minister in the reign of Charles II. and part of that of James II., whom he had betrayed by the basest treachery to William of Orange. "Since the Revolution (1688) Sunderland had striven to escape public observation in country retirement, but he came forward now with his plan for William"—who felt that something must be done to appease the appetite of parliament, because parliament that had made him, contrary to the constitution, could unmake him in the said manner. "His plan was to place all the power of the crown in parliament by choosing the ministers from the strongest faction in parliament." From that date the government became not the government of the empire, of the king, but of a faction; from that date (1697) the power of the crown became the jack-pot for the play of political parties; from that date, by the plan of a renegade, the loyalty of the ministry is pledged not to the crown and empire, but to the faction from whom they are chosen, while their oath of office to crown and constitution remains a constant perjury on their lips. Green's "Hist. of the English People" shows that this class in power in England carried corruption on by excesses throughout the entire administration.

Now while the Anglo-Amrican provinces made no great trouble over the change of dynasty, they refused to recognize in the slightest degree this participation of parliament in the government of the colonies,—even the best features of that government. And the worst features the provinces would not endure. In Ryerson's *"Loyalists of America,"* Vol. I., p. 473, it reads: "The Southern colonies with those of New England shared the same fate of misrepresentation, abuse and invasion of their rights as British subjects. The flames of discontent were spread through all the colonies by a set of incompetent and reckless governors, the favorites and tools of perhaps the worst administration and the most corrupt that ever ruled in Great Britain."

It is true the American colonies, especially the four

New England colonies, had been protected by Great Britain during all the past wars with the French in Canada, into which Great Britain had been drawn on their account.

For a period of seventy years the fleets and armies of England had been employed in the service of Massachusetts and her dependant off-shoots to save them from being "Driven into the sea." The debt of Great Britain, in consequence of these exertions, amounted in 1764 to £140,000,000 or $700,000,000.

Even in the struggle for their own preservation and security, what the colonies had contributed had been subject to the caprice of their legislatures.

Some of the colonies had made exertions "so far beyond their quota" as to be able to demand a reimbursement from the national treasury, which was accorded them; the other colonies had paid only part of the debt long after it was due, and who could compel them, and how was that compulsion to be enforced in the future?

The solution of the problem by parliamentary interference led to disturbance and to the final separation of the American colonies from Great Britain. Even Mr. Pitt, so long the friend of America, told Dr. Franklin that "When the war closed, if he should be in the ministry, he would take measures to prevent the colonies from having a power to refuse or delay the supplies that might be wanted for national purposes."

The first act of the British parliament to force the colonies to pay their part of the war debt was passed March 10th, 1764. It levied heavy duties on all articles brought into the colonies from the French and other West Indian islands, and ordered that these duties must be paid into the treasury of London in specie. Another bill was brought into parliament in the same session to "Restrain the currency of paper money in the colonies."

Popular meetings were held in the colonies, when the news of this reached them, to express indignation thereat. Associations resolved to abstain from the use of all articles imported on which duties were assessed, and to use only home-made goods.

But yet, when the colonists were excited to opposition they had no grounds for complaint against the right of the British Parliament to impose these duties, because regulation of affairs between the colonies and for the empire as a whole in commercial and external relations came under the rule of office of the London Parliament.

But parliament when it discovered that, through evasion and the non-use of articles of foreign make, very little money was raised, began to devise other means, and these means effected the internal arrangements of the colonies, which the colonists felt were infringements of the rights of their own legislatures and of their own charters of self-government. The chief bill of this description was introduced into parliament by Mr. Grenville, March 10th, 1765, to raise a revenue in the colonies by stamps which should be affixed to all newspapers, law papers, ship papers, property transfers, college diplomas and marriage licenses. A fine of £10 was imposed for non-compliance with the act. Jurisdiction was taken away from the local courts by this act and confined to the Courts of Admiralty without juries, the officers of which were appointed by the London Parliament, and who were paid fees out of fines imposed, the informer receiving one half.

Thus, by this act, the colonies felt that, not only were the rights conferred on them by charter interfered with and their local courts debarred from exercising power, but that the London Parliament, contrary to the constitution, was usurping the prerogative of the crown in America.

The legislative assembly of Massachusetts was dissolved by the royal governor Barnard because of its remonstrance, and also on account of a circular letter addressed by it to the other colonial legislatures. The Virginia House of Burgesses was also dismissed by the royal governor, Lord Botetout.

The British Parliament, however, in 1769, was brought to repeal 5s 6d of the duties on imported goods. But the next year, 1770, an affray occurred in the streets of Boston between some soldiers on duty and a mob of rioters who were creating a reign of terror. The British Parliament then made the governor and judges independent of all colonial power. These actions on the part of the British Parliament added to the hostility of the American colonists. It needed but a few more measures on both sides to change the latent hostility into strife.

In 1770 parliament allowed the East Indian Company of England to sell tea in the colonies free of duty, thereby depriving the American merchants of a share in the profits of that trade. The Americans throughout the years 1771-2 and 3 contented themselves with forming associations pledging themselves not to use the tea imported. These were the conditions in all the colonies. But in September, 1774, a Congress, composed of members sent by the citizens of all the colonies, met at Philadelphia to consider the state of affairs and what measures ought to be taken to correct them. An address was offered to the crown. It terminated with these words:— "Place us in the same situation that we were at the close of the late war, and our former harmony will be restored."

When the British Parliament met in January, 1774, there were laid before it, not only the papers from the Colonial Congress, but a number of letters from the royal governors and revenue and military officers, testifying to the spirit of opposition existing in the colonies against the unconstitutional acts of the London Parliament.

The consequence was, that, instead of renouncing the tax on the colonies, recalling the troops sent to coerce them and restoring to their courts and legislatures their proper functions, the English Parliament resolved to abate nothing of their vigor against the Americans until they yielded unconditionally. Moreover, parliament proceeded to pass an act to punish all of the New England colonies for their sympathy with Massachusetts, by restricting their trade with England and depriving them of Newfoundland fisheries.

In 1775 the General Assembly of New York adopted a memorial to present to the king, begging him to restore the charter to Massachusetts, which had been taken away, and to open the port of Boston which had been closed. The petition of New York was rejected by the British ministry without a hearing.

In the same year, 1775, the second Continental Congress met again at Philadelphia. All the colonies sent representatives but Georgia. The mission of this congress was to restore harmony in the colonies between the royal and local authorities and to obtain a redress of grievances.

A petition was framed by this congress and presented to the king. It, like all similar colonial documents of the period, abounded in expressions of loyalty and humbly prayed for just and constitutional usage such as was accorded them by their charters, whose rights were now infringed.

The petition sent by the Continental Congress, asking that the restrictions be removed, was ignominiously disregarded by parliament, and the colonists were termed rebels for exercising this constitutional right of protest. The royal officers in the colonies were commanded to seize the cannon and ammunition and small arms of the colonists.

The attempt of Gen. Gage, who commanded the British troops in Boston, to capture the stores of the colonists, thirty miles away, at Concord and Lexington, led to an engagement between the provincials and the king's troops, in which the stores were saved and lives were lost on both sides.

Lord Dunmore, governor of Virginia for the king, performed a similar hostile act by seizing the stores at Williamsburg in that colony. He was driven, however, by the armed forces of the Virginians to seek shelter on a British ship of war.

It was during this state of feeling that the Continental Congress reassembled on May 10th, 1776.

The delegates to this congress were nerved to more determined action by the knowledge of what had taken place in Massachusetts and Virginia, and by the fact that parliament had, in the preceding December, passed an act to increase the army and navy, and had hired 17,000 Hessian and Hanoverian troops to aid in reducing the colonies to submission. But the colonists would not recede from their demands, which were these: I. The right to tax themselves by their own elected representatives; II. The right of providing for the support of their own civil government and its officers; and III. Non-interference of parliament with crown functions in the provinces. These rights they had already enjoyed, according to the privilege of British citizenship and the provisions of their own charters, until these privileges and charters were taken away. The colonists declared that they would defend these rights and oppose with arms the enforcement of whatever was contrary to them.

CHAPTER II.

Consolidation on Constitutional Basis Against Parliamentary Usurpation Parties in the Colonies.

It had been the policy of the Stuarts, according to the feudal constitution, to create a confederacy—a federation of states—each independent of the others but in feudation to the king. England was but one of these states, although the principal one—the one in which was to be situated the general capital of the empire. In this system—which was the feudal system—the same on which rested the constitution of Britain and of all European states—the parliament of England had no more right to legislate for the Province of Virginia, or Maryland, than the parliament of Virginia or Maryland had to legislate for the Kingdom of England. In England the chief authority was the king and parliament; in Virginia it was the king and government of Virginia; in Massachusetts it was the king and government of Massachusetts, and likewise in each of the other provinces. For furtherance of the plan of federating the various states and principalities of his empire, King James II. had ordered in 1688—the very year that the Revolution in England prevented its execution—the confederation of the Northern colonies at Albany under the name of the "Dominion of New England." May 1, 1690, a congress of their representatives did meet to consider means for a common defence against the Indians, the New York members being Jacob Leister and Peter de La Noy. Another congress met in Albany for the same purpose in 1722. But these meetings were inspired by the encouragements given by the former Stuart kings as means of building up centres of power on the outskirts of the empire as well as for local needs and protection. But after the Revolution of 1688, when the London Parliament usurped crown functions and extended its withering, jealous and illegitimate authority to every province, blighting provincial life and expansion for the benefit of its own narrow constituency, these provincial confederations were discouraged.

In 1754 seven governors assembled at Albany, Province of New York, and signed a treaty of peace with the Iroquois Indians. At the same time they addressed the Home Government on the project of a federal union, whereby the force of the several colonies might be employed to act against a common enemy. This proposed government was to consist of a President appointed by the crown, and a general council commissioned by the provincial authorities. The President was to have executive authority, appoint all civil and military officers and act with his council legislatively. This government was to have power to make war and peace in America, and impose taxes with approval of the crown. The project was rejected by the English Parliament.

In 1778 Mr. Ogden, chief justice of New Jersey, suggested a government for America to have similar power, only its composition was to consist of a governor-general appointed by the crown, and a legislature to consist of a house of barons with hereditary privileges, created by the crown for honorable and meritorious families in the colonies, and a house of assembly elected by the freeholders of the population. The political disturbances existing in the colonies at that time prevented the entertainment of Mr. Ogden's proposition, but it is likely that the English Parliament would have viewed it with disfavor. David Ogden was at that time one of the Board of Delegates of the United Empire Loyalists and his proposition was advanced as a remedy for healing the wounds made by the English parliament in the Provincial understanding of constitutional government. The particular of his proposal provided that: "The right of taxation of America by the British Parliament be given up; that the several colonies be restored to their former constitutions and form of government. . . that each colony have a governor and council appointed by the Crown, and a house of representatives elected by the free-holders inhabiting the several counties . . who shall have power to make all necessary laws for the internal government and benefit of each colony that are not repugnant to the laws of Great Britain or the laws of the American Parliament . . that an American Parliament be established for all the English colonies on the continent to consist of a Lord-Lieutenant, Barons (to be created for the purpose), not to exceed for the present more than twelve nor less than eight, from the principles of each colony . . a House of Commons not to exceed twelve nor less than eight from each colony to be elected by the house of representatives of each colony . . that this American Parliament have supervision and government of the several colleges in North America, most of which have been the great nurseries of the late rebellion, instilling into the tender minds of youth principles unfavorable to monarchical government and favorable to republican and other doctrine incompatible with the British constitution."

But while the intelligent and conservative people were basing their opposition on an assertion of the constitution as a means of redress,—a constitution that the London Parliament was knawing and eating into by those rats of jurisprudence, the "fictions" of the English law— the demagogues and liberals of the colonies were stirring up the lower classes with democratic intent, for separation from the empire, the plunder of the royalists and the institution of a republic. From the time of the earliest Puritan settlements there had been a strong democratic inclination among the lower orders of the population and the extreme Congregationalists. This feeling, reënforced by religious prejudice, was hostile to monarchical institutions—notwithstanding that the Bible favors monarchy and Heaven is represented as a Kingdom. In 1704 Chief-Justice Montperron of New York wrote to the Earl of Nottingham that: "The inhabitants of Rhode Island conduct their affairs as though they were not of the British dominions." About the same time Lord Cornbury wrote to the London Board of Trade that the people of Connecticut bore "a great hatred towards those who held allegiance to the sovereign."

It is true that there were many arguments used to promote this feeling of hostility. Not the least of these were the restrictions placed by the London Parliament— since it had usurped royal functions in the colonies over barter and sale, commercial contracts and colonial manufactures. But the London Parliament, representing the English trading classes alone, could not be expected to use the royal prerogative over the colonies but to restrict the actions of the American trading classes for the benefit of its own constituency. America was not the constituency of the London parliament, but was a fief of the Crown.

It is true that the Crown had a claim on all ship timber and on all mines of coal and ore, none of which might be taken without the sovereign's permission. But this permission was granted for the benefit of the people and withheld only from speculators and exploiters. The Crown in this matter acts but as trustee for the people's lands, and it would be better for Canada were this trusteeship not so much rat-eaten by legal fictions—for, by the delegation of authority to a parliamentary ministry—responsible not to the Crown—but to parliament—a corrupt party in power is continually robbing the real estate of the country—of the Crown—to enrich itself.

The slighting of colonial petitions by the London Parliament from 1763 to 1775, which petitions were for constitutional observance in the government of the empire, and the indifference manifested towards the people of the colonies by the partizans of the House of Hanover, raised a yet stronger feeling in the colonies against the home government.

The more southern colonies did not suffer directly as did those of the North by this action of the London Parliament, although their charters were threatened, but the Northern colonies, early attached to a Puritanical democracy, were studious to enflame resentment in the South, so the better to carry out the secret intent of revolution. These democrats in the North, anxious to "get rich quick" at some other person's expense, confused the position occupied by the honest and aristocratic who were attached to the constitution. Here was their method of procedure: "They proposed in the legislature (of Massachusetts) various schemes for bolstering up the depreciated currency. . . One of these was a Land Bank, which was actually established. About 800 people, among whom was the father of Sam. Adams, were incor-

porated with power to issue bills on security, chiefly of real estate" . . (beginning of the scheme of Yankee capitalization frauds). "This enterprise made confusion worse confounded. The securities were usually of little value and the Land Bank bills were refused utterly by the better classes to the great wrath of the populace." . .
"In 1738 the paper money party in town-meeting proposed that Boston's representatives in the General Court be instructed to favor the emission of more paper money. Hutchinson (the Tory delegate) promptly refused to be bound by such a mandate. . . When his house caught fire some of the people on the street shouted, "Curse him, let it burn." . .

"In 1749 the English Parliament voted that a large sum of money should be paid the Massachusetts colony as compensation for its expenditures in the recent capture of Louisbourg. Hutchinson proposed that this money should be used to redeem and cancel the paper currency of the colony." . . "By his force of argument Hutchinson carried the measure through the House against what had been a majority in favor of irredeemable paper money. The Governor and Council (Royalists) promptly approved of the measure and it became a law. All over the colony there was an outcry of wrath. Hutchinson was in danger of personal violence and was defeated for reëlection. Within a year, however, the blessings of a fixed and stable currency and the consequent improvement of business became so obvious that Hutchinson's conduct was loudly praised and censure ceased except among those who had hoped to turn a dishonest penny by the steady decrease in the values of paper money."—(From the sketch of *"Thomas Hutchinson, the Tory Governor of Massachusetts,"* by President Charles H. Levermore of Adelphi College, Brooklyn, in the February, 1902, number of the *New England Magazine*). The financial policy of the United States began here and was the oil on the fire of the Revolution, the appetite in the belly of the Demon. It is said that there is "nothing in a name." The lie is no more potently expressed than in the difference between honest, old-fashioned and legal "mortgage" and the dishonest, revolution-bred and illegitimate "capitalization." To work an estate, a man can by law mortgage it to others for two-thirds its value, so that the mortgages have a legitimate security. But several people are allowed to join their estates into a company and sell stock "capitalized" to the extent of ten and sometimes a hundred, yea, and in the United States often to a thousand times their value; and in the course of time "put their company into the hands of a receiver," fail up, and retire (limited) worth several millions each, leaving their creditors with the "capitalized stock," not worth a dollar. That there should be a law-decision that capitalized industries may be raised to but two-thirds of their actual value, like any other mortgaged estate, is evident—even if they are on a paying basis. And they are *not* on a paying basis until they monopolize the market by shutting out, through legislation, similar products. Then their per cent. payments are not due from their own industries but from the tribute of high prices wrung from the entire people by concurrence of a corrupt and purchased legislature. It was for the accomplishment of such things as these which the restraint of crown and aristocracy forbade in the colonies, that fostered the Revolutionary party.

"Hutchinson's hostility to a paper currency had fixed a deep gulf between him and the more democratic element among his neighbors. The chasm had been widened by his opposition in 1757 to the creation of Danvers as a separate township, principally because an increase of representatives would give the House (democratic) an undue influence in legislation."

"One of Hutchinson's first acts as chief-justice was destined to increase the alienation between him and the populace. He was called on to decide whether the Superior Court could issue lawfully writs of assistance to customs officers in their search for smuggled goods." . .

"Hutchinson (himself) was opposed to any close scrutiny by the British government into the trade of the colonies, but he decided this question, moderately, wisely and loyally in the only way in which a judge sworn to interpret and obey the law could decide it." . .

"Hutchinson wrote: 'This trial (about writs of assistance) and my pernicious principles about the currency have taken away a great number of friends and the

House have not only reduced the allowance to the Superior Court, but have refused to make any allowance at all to me as chief-justice.'" . . .

"Against the enforcement of the Sugar Acts (of the London Parliament), which would destroy the New England trade with the West Indies, he had protested publicly and privately. His letters to English correspondents pleaded against that policy and against the Stamp Act." . . . "In spite of all this it was on Hutchinson that the worst violence of the Boston mob fell."

"That mob was the most thoroughly organized rabble in the Colonies. It consisted largely of the seamen and artisans who lived along the water front. Their immediate leader was a shoemaker named Mackintosh, a coarse and reckless fellow. The men who directed him and his lieutenants were Sam. Adams, William Cooper and other leading spirits of the far-famed Caucus Club. This club was the local Tammany. John Adams yields us a few glimpses of its operations as its members sat smoking and drinking in Adjutant Thomas Dawes's garret, parcelling out the local offices as a sort of nominating convention, and inculcating a strict obedience to what we would now call 'the machine.' To this compact body of workers, a background of respectability was furnished by the Merchants' Club, wherein men like Richard Dana, John Hancock (the smuggler), and James Otis, worked with Sam. Adams (the dishonest ex-tax collecter). . . . These were the managers who were ultimately responsible for the destruction of Hutchinson's house. In that house were depositions against certain merchants of Boston who were accused of smuggling . . . and the records of the Admiralty Courts which had cognizance of such cases. Some of the usual leaders of the populace undoubtedly knew who had spread the false report that Hutchinson had favored the Stamp Act." . . .

"On Monday evening (26 Aug., 1765) Mackintosh collected his gang about a bon-fire on State Street. They had liquor to drink, but desiring further inspirations, they broke into the cellars belonging to two royal officers and consumed all the liquors therein. Thus fortified, these 'Sons of Liberty' betook themselves to Hutchinson's house in Garden Court Street. He and his children had barely time to escape to a neighboring house. . . . Hutchinson's letter describes this:—

"'The hellish crew fell on my house with the rage of devils and in a moment split down the doors and entered. My son being in the great entry, heard them cry, 'Damn him, he is upstairs; we'll have him!' . . . 'Not content with tearing off all the wainscot and hangings, and splitting the doors to pieces, they beat in the partition walls . . . cut down the cupola . . . and began to take the slate and boards from the roof but were prevented by approaching daylight. . . The garden house was laid flat and all my trees broken to the ground. . . Besides my plate and family pictures household furniture of every kind, my own, my children's and servants' apparel, they carried off about £900 sterling and emptied the house of everything whatsoever. . . They have scattered or destroyed all the MSS. and other papers I had been collecting for 30 years, besides a great number of public papers in my custody.'"

"During the riot one of the militia officers observed two men disguised, with long staves in their hands, who acted as directors. He ventured to say to them that the Lieutenant-Governor might not be the only one injured by the destruction of so many papers. Answer was made that it had been resolved to destroy everything in the house, and such would be carried out." . . .

"For weeks and months the leaders of the democracy governed the town by a system of espionage and terrorism, boycotting tradesmen not favorable to them, mobbing the persons or houses or both of those who censured them, and maintaining a sort of Holy Inquisition into the daily business of counting-rooms and the daily contents of kitchens. Gov. Hutchinson doubted his right to call out the troops. . . He exhorted the justices to act. They replied that the assemblies might be unwarrantable, but there were times when irregularities could not be restrained. . . Had either Bernard or Hutchinson used the regiments with proper vigor the Mackintoshes would never have dared to stain the cause of liberty and that conflict between the citizens and soldiers, miscalled the

'Boston Massacre,' would never have occurred." (Levermore's "*Gov. Hutchinson,*" N. Eng. Magazine, Feb., 1901.)

This mob and its leaders so well described by Levermore was the counterpart of other mobs existing in the colonies from whose organizations have sprung the government of the republic of the United States and its existing society. Sam. Adams, its leader, had been dismissed from the British civil service as a dishonest collector of taxes. And he has described John Hancock (the smuggler) "as an ape, Robert Treat Paine as an ox, and Cushing as an ass." The entire scheme of these "Sons of Liberty" was to liberate themselves from parliamentary authority for the sake of the plunder and proscription of the great provincial families. An U. E. Loyalist officer of Georgia said: "They are vermin who seek to drive out the old families." To accomplish this, their leaders, the "smartest rascals" in the colonies, seized on the justice of the cause, namely, that the provinces are not constituencies of the London Parliament, but are fiefs of the Crown, over which parliament has no legal jurisdiction. They hoped after embroiling all the colonies to call in foreign aid by means of which the Crown itself might be separated from its provincial fiefs, which would fall a prey to the democracy contrary to all the previous oaths of allegiance and spurious pretentions of its leaders.

CHAPTER III.

Conspiracy and Hypocrisy and Loyalty and Honor Armed Together.

For the holy purpose of defending the Crown and provincial constitution against the illegal action of the London Parliament the republicans and loyalists were united. But apart from this the republicans conspired among themselves to revolutionize society, plunder the aristocracy and overturn the state. Without foreign aid they could not do this. They had been told that France was desirous for revenge against England for the loss of Canada and Louisiana and they began overtures to France at the very time that they were protesting their loyalty to Britain. One of them, Dr. Franklin, whom the French called "Bonhomme," said in 1773, "I never heard from any person the least expression of a wish for separation." Oct., 1774, Washington wrote: "I am well satisfied that no such thing as independence is desired by any thinking man in America." April, 1775, Jefferson wrote: "I never heard whisper of a disposition to separate from Great Britain," and "as for the form of the British government, it is the best yet and I desire none better" (to Sir John Randolph). At the same time John Adams published in Boston: "That there are any who pant after independence is the greatest slander in the province."

Ryerson (*"Loyalists of America,"* Vol. I., p. 513) says: "It seems difficult to recognize with truthfulness, fairness and consistency the intrigues and proposed terms of alliance between the leaders of Congress and the King of France. These intrigues commenced . . . while the authors of them were disclaiming any wish or design, to separate from England and their desire to be reconciled with the mother-country by a recognition of their rights as they existed before 1763."

"As early as Dec., 1775 . . . a secret committee of correspondence of Congress wrote Arthur Lee, their agent in London, and Charles Dumas, at The Hague, requesting them to ascertain the feeling of European Courts respecting America, enjoining them to 'great circumspection and secrecy.'"

"M. de Beauvoulois, agent for the French government, appeared in Philadelphia, held a secret conference with the secret committee and assured them that France was ready to aid the colonies on such conditions as might be considered equitable. These conferences were so secret that M. de Beauvoulois said that, 'the committee met him at an appointed place after dark, each going to it by a different road.' A few weeks later Silas Deane, by the secret committee, was appointed commercial agent to Europe to obtain supplies and to communicate to the French premier, Comte de Vergennes, the probable separation from Great Britain."

After once being known is it possible that dependence can be put on a nation sprung from such material? Gen. Wolfe had written in his day: "The Americans are in general the dirtiest, most contemptible, cowardly dogs that you can conceive. There is no depending on 'em in action. They fall down dead in their own dirt and desert by battalions, officers and all. Such rascals as these are rather an encumbrance than a strength."

Washington, who had been used to better things in the society of the Fairfaxes, Brockinboroughs, Randolphs, Grymeses and other royalists of Virginia, wrote in Nov., 1775, about these new people of the democracy: "Such a dearth of public spirit and such a want of virtue, such stock-jobbing and fertility in all the low arts to obtain advantages of one kind or another I never saw before and pray God's mercy that I may never see again!"

At this time and up to 1778, the time when the London Parliament ate humble pie and acknowledged that the provinces were not its constituencies, but were fiefs of the Crown with whose management it had no right to interfere, the major part of the royalists as well were united in opposition to it. The bravest and most resolute organized themselves as "Minute Men" under three articles: I. To defend the Royal Prerogative in the province. II. To defend the provincial constitution. III. To obey their own officers chosen by themselves to these ends. Colonists of all classes, royalists and republicans, sent delegates to a congress to form means of defense. Each colony provided for the enlistment of its own militia. And in many instances the militia of different colonies refused to leave the territory of their particular colony because they had been recruited merely to defend that territory. All officers below the rank of Colonel were appointed by the provincial government, while the general officers were commissioned by Congress.

But there were more republicans, who had an understanding among themselves, than royalists, in the Congress of 1775. They were arranged as follows:—

The delegates of the Northern colonies in the General Congress at Philadelphia in 1775, were for separating from the Empire. The delegates of the six southern colonies were for resisting the infringement of their charters by the action of the London Parliament, but preferred to remain in the Empire, and with a royal form of government. Pennsylvania, the thirteenth colony, had five delegates. Of these two were for separating from the Empire, two were for the Empire and royalty, and the fifth man undecided. The republicans saw their chance here. Disguising their intent they, under the plea of forming parliamentary rules to expedite affairs, urged three measures, which were adopted by all the delegates. These measures were:—

I. That the Congress should count votes by colonies.

II. That the majority of the delegates of a colony should control the voice of that colony.

III. That what a majority of the colonial voices thus constituted should decide to do, the others would be bound to follow.

Measures from this time forward went pretty much as the republicans directed, for the wavering of the fifth vote of Pennsylvania was intrigued for by them. When the motion was put that the colonies be declared Free and Independent States, the six southern colonies voted against the measure. The six northern colonies voted for it, and three of the five votes that Pennsylvania had, turned the balance by making that colony on the side of separation and democracy. Hence Pennsylvania is called the "Keystone State." The vote then stood by colonies, seven for separation and democracy, and six for Empire and royalty. The intrigue that gained the one vote of Pennsylvania that turned the balance in favour of separation, imposed on the unwilling southern colonies the burden of assisting in a cause for which their delegates had been led to pledge their honour, before the ultimate purpose of that cause was revealed to them. It is true that the Cavaliers who had fought for the Stuarts from the time of Charles I. in the middle of the 17th century to the time of Charles Edward, the "Pretender's" son, in the middle of the 18th, and had taken refuge in the colonies, bore no greater love for the House of Hanover, now seated on the British throne, than the Puritans, whose sires had crossed the ocean to found a government without priestcraft and kingcraft. The Scottish and Irish families from Ulster, who had come to the colonies to be freed from a parliamentary jurisdiction in Ireland that debarred them from public position and representation if they were not of the Established Church, were also determined to resist the imposition of a parliamentary tyranny in the colonies. Another class, the exiled knight-errants of Europe, like De Kalb, Kusiosko, Pulaski, and De Elbe, saw in the formation of a new state the opportunity of winning feudal tenures by strengthening the sword of Washington. Finally, those whose families had won a way in the New World burned with the desire to resent the slights cast on their achievements and pretensions.

It is true that the colonists had charters from the Crown, but they had created the power on which their governments rested, and they had made states where before there were deserts. In the heat of mutual recrimination many were borne beyond their cooler calculations, and were led by crafty democrats to come to a rupture with the Home Government instead of a reconciliation.

That same year (1775) Lord Chatham brought forward a bill in parliament to reconcile the two parties by withdrawing parliamentary interference with colonial affairs, but it was defeated. The news of this defeat put the colonies at once under arms.

Immediately, the armed ports, mostly under surveillance of colonial authorities in their various territories, were occupied. Large forts and arsenals that were not securely guarded fell into the same hands without a struggle. Only one colony refused to act with the others in this matter, and that was the Colony of Georgia. Although a party existed there favorable to an union with the other colonies, it did not develop an early strength, and after it did come to an expression it was speedily extinguished, while the loyal Province of Florida, that had been acquired from Spain, poured her troops over the border, under command of Gen. Prevost, and quelled all further uprisings until the final surrender of the province by Lord Cornwallis in the terms following on the surrender at Yorktown in 1782.

There were small conflicts here and there in all the colonies, as the colonial authorities proceeded to gather the means of defense, but none so serious as that at Concord and Lexington in Massachusetts.

For quite a while powder, shot and arms had been collected in the neighborhood of Concord and Lexington, and the first serious effort made by the metropolitan troops to dispossess the locality of these stores brought on the beginning of the American Revolution.

Lord Percy's letters show the British side of this account, and, as the American side of the story is known to every schoolboy, the British side will be novel and interesting, especially as Lord Percy was an eyewitness of the greater part of the fight, he having been sent with the relief corps from Boston to cover the retreat of the Concord and Lexington expedition.

It seems that Lieutenant-Colonel Smith, at the head of nearly 800 grenadiers, light infantry and marines, marched to Lexington and Concord, dispersed the few militia who were posted there, destroyed some of the military stores which had not been removed by the inhabitants to places of greater safety, and started on their return trip to Boston. But at this time bodies of armed men arrived from every quarter; the woods were full of them, so were housetops, barns, from which an incessant fire was kept up on the British force. The peril of this force was great, and General Gage sent Lord Percy with reinforcements to save them. The following is Percy's official account to General Gage:—

"Sir,—In obedience to your Excellency's orders, I marched yesterday (April 19), at 9 o'clock in the morning, with the First Brigade and two field pieces, in order to cover the retreat of the grenadiers and light infantry on their return from the expedition to Concord.

"As all the houses were shut up, and there was not the appearance of a single inhabitant, I could get no intelligence concerning them till I had passed Menotomy (Brookline), where I was informed that the rebels had attacked his Majesty's troops, who were retiring, overpowered by numbers, greatly exhausted and fatigued, and having expended almost all their ammunition. And about 2 o'clock I met them retiring through the town of Lexington.

"I ordered immediately the two field pieces to fire at the rebels, and drew up the brigade on a height. The shot from the cannon had the desired effect and stopped the rebels for a little time, who dispersed and endeavored to surround us, being very numerous. Now, as it began to grow pretty late, and we had 15 miles to retire and only our 36 rounds, I ordered the grenadiers and light infantry to move off first and covered them with my brigade, sending out very strong flanking parties, which was absolutely necessary, as there was not a stone wall or house, though before in appearance evacuated, from whence the rebels did not fire on us.

"So soon as they saw us begin to retire, they pressed very much on our rear guard, which for that reason I relieved every now and then. In this manner we retired for 15 miles under an incessant fire all around us till we arrived at Charlestown between 7 and 8 in the evening, very much fatigued with a march of about 30 miles and having expended almost all our ammunition.

"We had the misfortune of losing a good many men in the retreat, though nothing like the number which from many circumstances I have reason to believe were killed of the rebels.

"His Majesty's troops during the whole affair behaved with their usual intrepidity and spirit. Nor were

they a little exasperated at the cruelty and barbarity of the rebels, who scalped and cut off the ears of some of the wounded men who fell into their hands. I am, etc.,
(Signed) "PERCY,
"Acting Brigadier-General."

In another letter to General Harvey he says: "During the whole affair the rebels attacked us in a very scattered, irregular manner, but with perseverance and resolution, nor did they ever dare to form into any regular body. Indeed, they knew too well what was proper to do so.

"Whoever looks on them as an irregular mob will find himself much mistaken. They have men among them who know very well what they are about, having been employed as rangers against the Indians and Canadians, and this country being much covered by wood and hilly, is very advantageous for their method of fighting.

"Nor are several of their men void of a spirit of enthusiasm, as we experienced yesterday, for many of them concealed themselves in houses and advanced to within 10 yards to fire at me and other officers, though they were morally certain of being put to death themselves in an instant.

"You may depend on it that, as the rebels have now had time to prepare, they are determined to go through with it, nor will the insurrection here turn out so despicable as it is imagined perhaps at home."

It was at this time that some of the Puritan Yankees who dominated in the former "Land of Evangeline" met together in a church in Nova Scotia to prepare an organization of sympathy and of aid for the democrats of the old colonies. They were filled with hatred for the French, whose land had been robbed from them and on which land they were now living. They were exasperated to think that the French noblesse, the French language and the Catholic religion were confirmed in constitutional rights by the Act of Quebec of 1774.

But while they were deliberating on their treasonable projects, there stalked in among them an old soldier in full uniform with loaded and bayoneted musket. He had been retired and had settled in the neighborhood and had come to the meeting to act his part as a feudatory of the crown. Proceeding up the aisle, in the midst of the astounded Yankees, he reached the speaker's desk, which was vacated on his approach. Then turning about with his musket cocked and on guard, he demanded in a loud voice for the man to rise who was plotting treason to the Crown and Constitution. At the sound of that demand there was an immediate scramble for the door, from which the conspirators scattered in safety for their homes. And the old soldier in his scarlet uniform, on guard to defend the constitution and the law, remained the triumphant master of the situation.

CHAPTER IV.

Struggles in the Field.

The 10th of May is the anniversary of the capture of Ticondiroga and Crown Point by Cols. Allen, Arnold and Warner in the year 1775. They were the three "Black Crows" of the Northern Border.

There remains yet a stone bastion and part of the walls of this ancient colonial fortress, green grown with the moss and lichens of an hundred and fifty years. There is yet the outlines of a redoubt, stretching across the field where the Highlanders of Abercrombie's British army pressed forward, where Montcalm's intrepid French formed in line behind earthern defense, against which the British broke in vain. This fort which had been built by the Baron Dieskau in 1755, when Canada was prosperous beneath the ever-glorious golden lilies of France, was lifted up by the waters of Lake Champlain as the "gateway of Canada." From it there issued the few but valorous troops of France against the English possessions further south, penetrating at one time to Albany, which they burned. Towards it had marched by mountains, plain and shore the 16,000 veteran and provincial troops of Abercrombie of 1757. The next year the fort was abandoned by the French, and after Canada had passed to England by the Treaty of 1763, the fort was enlarged and strengthened by Lord Amherst, who built a road from it to Crown Point. The British officials, with their usual carelessness, did not seem to think that this fort with its 200 canon and immense quantities of supplies in 1775 would be an easy prey to the American colonists, for it was garrisoned by but 42 men commanded by Capt. Delaplace and a lieutenant. Crown Point had but 12 men under a sergeant, and the fort by Lake George was occupied only by the caretaker and his wife!

In 1773 Gen. Haldimand, a Swiss mercenary in the pay of England, chief military authority in that part of the country, reported that there was no need of more than a nominal garrison. Because neither he thought, nor his fellows, that the American colonies would rebel against the Crown, however much they might "talk" rebellion.

Now there was one, John Brown, of Pittsfield, Mass., who had a secret mission to Montreal in March, 1775—where some English deserters were ready to join any attempt against the Crown that might happen. They were some of those who opened the gates of Montreal afterwards to Montgomery and furnished what is known as the 1st Canadian Regiment to Montgomery's invading army.

This Mr. Brown was astonished at the stupidity of the English in leaving such a feeble garrison over the "Gateway of Canada." He wrote to Sam. Adams and Dr. Warren, who were on the "committee of correspondence" of the colony, and the capture of Tricondiroga was planned. On the 20th of April, Benedict Arnold, on the way to Cambridge with a company of volunteers, learned of the defenseless condition of the fort also, and of the great number of cannon and muskets and the abundance of warlike material there, and he started immediately with his company for the place.

At the same time for the capture of the same place, the hunters, squatters on disputed land and the house-raiders and barn-burners of the Green Mountains, under their notorious leader, "Col." Ethen Allen, were forming their plans, over their whiskey pots and tobacco pipes, in Catamount Tavern. And while all this was going on about them, while companies were arming in every colony to fight against the British, the English officials, with a stupidity that is amazing, took no heed.

The troops of Arnold met those of Allen on the road, and there arose immediately a dispute between these worthies about the command. They swore at each other; they damned each other's eyes; they accused each other of scheming to be dictators if not kings, until Allen, whose followers were more numerous, turned to his second officer, Amos Callender, and roared: "What shall I do with the damned rascal? Shall I put him under guard?" Callender replied, advising them to share the "honors" equally and both lead. And so peace was restored, although the two "Colonels" looked at each other out of the corners of their eyes and chewed their wrath with their tobacco.

When they arrived at the fort, which was just "at the dawn of day," when the mist was rising like a thin ghost from a mighty shroud, the sleepy sentry did not perceive them until they were within the gate. He could not give the alarm by firing a shot, for in "that piping time of peace" he had not thought it necessary to load his gun. He rushed into the fort, followed by Arnold and Allen and their 300 men, who were obliged even then to shout and cheer before they succeeded in awakening the sleeping English garrison, who appeared soon in shirt-tails and rubbed their eyes in amazement.

Allen enquired of them where was their leader and they replied "a-bed." So Allen clambered up the stairway to the Captain's room, and, after a great pounding on the door, was successful in awakening him. When Capt. Delaplace came out, he was attired like his soldiers, in a shirt-tail, but he wore a greater mark of distinction in a night-cap, with a little silk tassel. He told Allen that he disapproved of such an early call and demanded to know his business. Allen replied that he had come to demand the surrender of the fort, at the same time he waved an old cutlass which he carried and made other demonstrations to prove that he was in earnest. Capt. Delaplace refused to look the matter seriously in the face, and believed that Allen was speaking in a Pickwickian sense (although then Mr. Dickens had not thought of Mr. Pickwick), or in modern phrase, he believed that Allen was "talking through his hat," and he demanded by what authority. With another wave of his cutlass, and in a voice that had been tuned to a dominant key in the disputes of Catamount Tavern, Allen shouted, "In the name of the Great Jehovah and the Continental Congress." Before this sacred alliance, to prove which Allen pointed to his 300 "Angels" below, Capt. Delaplace was forced to yield. At this moment, after all the glory had been gathered in, Col. Warner arrived with another troop of armed men, and the remaining places, Crown Point and the fort of Lake George, were taken.

Thus, without any other disturbance than the awakening of the little garrison and the spoiling of the commandant's appetite for breakfast, the greatest arsenal of arms and ammunition outside of the citadel of Quebec was transferred on that day from the authority of the King of England to that of "The Great Jehovah and the Continental Congress" as proclaimed by "Col." Ethan Allen, and, although the "Great Jehovah" is not mentioned in the Constitution, yet a little later he was put on the coinage, "In God we trust."

In the meantime Col. George Washington had been appointed commander-in-chief of the united forces of all the colonies by the Continental Congress holding session in Philadelphia. Washington took command of the troops of the several colonies at Cambridge assembled, just before the Battle of Bunker's Hill, June 17th, 1776. He found that most of the men assembled had had previous military experience under the British colonial authority against the French and Indians and knew therefore how to fire a gun to advantage. Their courage and energy had been fortified by monarchical institutions, of whose king, whose former troops they were, they were assembled to fight. They had arms and munitions in abundance, and cannon from the several small forts which they had captured in the interior. But the ethical value of the men was of little account. The annals of that time offer a startling lesson to the present. "Desertions of 20 and 30 happened very frequently, many of whom fled to Maine and Vermont and were among the settlers of those states at that time." "One thousand men, the date of whose enlistment was lost, perjured themselves in a body . . . in order to quit the ranks they had joined voluntarily." "Many enlisted, deserted and reënlisted, under other recruiting officers, so as to get double bounty." "Some prowled about the country to rob and kill the unoffending and defenseless." Gen. Knox wrote to Gerry that there were "men in commission who had been rewarded with rank without having any pretension to it except through cabal and intrigue." "Some of these were clamorous for more pay, while they drew large sums of public money under pretext of paying their men, but applied them to the support of their own extravagance; some went home on furlough and never returned; some violated their paroles and were threatened by Washington with being exposed in every newspaper in the land . . . and so numerous were the convictions that their names were sent to Congress in lists." "Many of the surgeons," said Washington, "are very great rascals, often countenancing the men to sham complaints to avoid doing duty and receiving bribes for such certificates, for procuring such discharges or furloughs." In a letter to one of the governors, he asserted that the officers that that state sent him were "generally of the lowest class of the people and led their men to plunder the inhabitants and into every kind of mischief. In another letter to Gen. Lee, while he was at Cambridge, he describes the small sense of honor among the officers. To his brother, John Augustine Washington, he wrote that the officers nominated "were not fit to be bootblacks." This condition was not confined to the New England troops and their officers, but extended to other colonial officials. Washington in a letter to a member of Congress from Virginia, in 1778, declares "that 90 officers of the Virginia Line had conspired to resign and desert in a body."

Of the Generals, eighteen retired during the war; one for drunkenness, one to escape trial for drawing double pay, one deserted to the enemy, and the rest because of old age. In 1777, John Adams wrote: "I am weary to death of the wrangles between the military officers, high and low . . they quarrel like cats and dogs . . . scrambling for higher rank and more pay like apes for nuts."

Such was their general condition when Washington was called to the command at Cambridge, and in addition, they were looking forward to obtaining the plunder of the estates of those who were true to the Crown. There were some, however, who were not influenced by so base motives, but acted from resentment and hatred of the royalists, and others—a few extreme idealists—who dreamed of establishing an utopian republic with a commingling of the equality of the Athenian democracy with the majesty of the Roman dominion and with the doctrine of the liberty of the French philosophers of the 17th century, an impossible creation likely to result as results the experiment of commingling fire with powder.

And so to Cambridge the various colonies directed the men enlisted in their cause until the number assembled there amounted to over 14,000 of all arms. Among them were the New Hampshire troops, who had effected the capture of Fort William Henry, and on the road to them was coming a great deal of the ammunition, being drawn over the country roads in ox-carts. All these troops began to try and besiege the city of Boston, where lay encamped a portion of the British, while in the harbor was anchored some British men-of-war.

June 17th, the Continental Forces that had been ordered the day before to entrench themselves on Bunker's Hill, by mistake took up position on Breed's Hill and erected a strong redoubt. By the dawning light of the 17th, the British saw the position of the Americans and opened a fire from their battleships. At noon they landed 3,000 men in heavy marching order under the command of Gen. Howe and advanced towards Breed's Hill, where the Americans lay entrenched. A few of the Americans who dwelt in Boston were loyal to the Crown. Among them was a Mr. Willard who was serving under Lord Howe. He had a personal acquaintance with Col. Prescott, who was commanding the colonial position. Gen. Howe handed Willard the field-glass and asked him if he thought Prescott would fight. After a long gaze at the hard outlines of Prescott's face, Willard replied: "Yes sir, he will fight to the gates of hell." "Then," said Howe, "we will give him hell, itself," and forthwith he ordered a general advance.

Previous to this, Gen. Howe had believed that the entire body of Americans, although with grievances against the parliament, were too much attached to their motherland to do more than threaten a resistance. This was the general belief of all the high officials and dignitaries of the Crown. This was why the first military operations of the British were conducted so slowly—in order to give the Americans time "to repent and return to their allegiance."

As the order came for the troops to advance, the guns from the warships began to thunder on the American redoubts and pour red-hot shot into Charlestown, so that under cover of the smoke of the conflagration the troops might go up the hill somewhat hidden. As the British deployed into column of attack, partly concealed by the smoke of Charlestown, Howe ordered up his cannon to fire on the retrenchments. For some strange cause no cannon shot responded to the command. The reason for it was this: Mr. Lovell, the ordinance officer, was so much in love with the daughter of the schoolmaster of the regiment that he was confused about everything that day, and on this occasion, sent to the front 24lb. shot for 12lb. guns. The result was that the cannon were useless. A verse of the time commemorates this exploit in the following manner:—

"Our conductor, he got broke
For his misconduct sure, sir.
The shot he sent for 12lb. guns
Were made for 24, sir."

Sir William Howe, in a letter written subsequent to the attack on Breed's Hill, refers to this incident as the principle cause for the first British repulse. For the Americans were enabled by the lack of British artillery fire in front, to remain undisturbed behind their entrenchments and discharge their volleys at close range into the approaching ranks of the British. A second attack was repulsed in the same manner. But the third time the officers urged on the troops; the ships' batteries and field artillery renewed their protecting fire. It has been claimed that at this epoch the powder of the Americans gave out and they retired a space on their reserves. But it was their ability to hold the place that was lacking and they fled as the British climbed the hill. The Connecticut troops left their muskets sticking through the fence-rails behind which they were drawn up and ran without firing a shot, while their commander, Gen. Israel Putnam, swore like a mad-man as he ran after them and tried to rally them.

There was in the rear a strong reserve of New Hampshire men and the ox-carts, laden with powder and other munitions had arrived the very day of the British attack. Not only were the reserves supplied with powder enough for the battle, but they had enough remaining to fill the horns of Washington's entire army. The American forces retired to Prospect Hill and the British occupied Bunker's Hill. The loss of the British were 1,200 killed and wounded. The Americans acknowledged 500 killed and wounded and 5 cannon captured by the enemy.

But the Metropolitan troops did not pursue their success and the Colonial troops coming in all the time from distant colonies drew nearer and laid Boston under siege. Boston was cordoned by the republican army, and the cordon had been drawn closer since the battle of Bunker Hill. The British garrison, supported by a few loyalists, held the town, which had become a place of refuge for other loyalists who had resided in the vicinity, who had been true to the crown, even in the midst of armed opposition, preferring to abandon all rather than yield. Before April 20th, 1775, Gen. Gage, the British commander, wrote the Provincial Congress, asking that these loyalists in the surrounding towns be permitted to enter Boston with their effects. April 30th, the Provincial Congress granted such permission, and stationed officers at the Neck of Boston and Charlestown to secure their unmolested entrance. At this time one of the protests against the republicans by some loyalists said: "You make the air resound with the cry of liberty, but subject those who differ with you to the most outrageous tyranny."

Among the loyalists who availed themselves of this permission was Lady Frankland, widow of Sir Charles H. Frankland. Her story is one of the romances of American history. Her maiden name was Agnes Surriage, and at the age of 15 she was living with her parents at Marblehead. According to the chronicles of the time, they were "poor but decent folk."

It was at this time that Sir Charles Frankland was collector of customs at Boston, an office more sought for than that of Governor, on account of the perquisites attached thereto, although the salary was only $500 per annum.

Sir Charles was born at Bengal, where his father was Governor of the East Indian Company's possessions. His mother was the youngest and favorite daughter of the great Cromwell.

At the age of 25 Frankland was appointed collector of Boston. His winning and generous manner made him a favorite very soon in the "vice-regal" society of the town. He was a liberal patron of King's Chapel and of Harvard College.

But now comes to his meeting with Agnes. On a beautiful day in May, in 1742, Agnes was in the little front garden of her home in Marblehead, when Sir Charles drove by in his coach. Her dress was very short, for at that time she had outgrown it, and there was no more cloth in the house to piece it down. She had taken off her shoes and stockings, and her dress coming only to her knees showed the rarest and richest contour. Frankland, who had an artist's eye and soul, was not insensible to her beauty. In fact, he was struck dumb and tingled with admiration, as he paused at the garden gate, and began to converse with Agnes, who looked at him with the eyes of unabashed yet respectful familiarity. After Frankland had caressed her flowing hair and patted her lovely rounded arms, he gave her a half-crown with which to buy a pair of shoes. Then he departed, promising himself to see her again.

And the picture of dear Agnes did not leave his mind. Every day she came chasing through his thoughts, the sunbeams playing with her hair and the breezes blowing her dress away from her gracefully modelled limbs. He dreamed of her. So again, shortly thereafter, he found himself on the road to Marblehead, before the sweet, short-skirted Agnes. "Why did you not buy some shoes?" he said to Agnes, as he looked with warming pleasure at the yet bare and rosy limbs. "I did,'" replied Agnes, "but I keep them to wear Sundays." Then she gave him such a shy but witching glance that he could restrain himself no longer. He clasped her in his arms and kissed her. Then he entered the house and demanded permission of her parents to take her to Boston with him, he promising to educate her. The permission was obtained very easily; the poor folk saw the advantage it would be to Agnes to be under the protection of so great a man, and Agnes travelled back in the Frankland coach, with armorial on panel, and coachman and outrider.

Now Frankland was so much in love with Agnes that he could not let her remain at school. He built an elegant house at Hopkinton, 25 miles from Boston, and there, in the midst of a magnificent estate, and attended by 20 servants, he kept her as his very own. There were many loyalists in Hopkinton, and they had a jolly time, with love among the roses. In 1858 this house was occupied by Mr. Hildreth.

In 1754, Frankland visited England and took Agnes with him. The next year they were in Lisbon, at the time of the terrible earthquake. The day of this happening, Frankland and Agnes were riding through one of the streets of that city. A house fell on them, and they were buried beneath the ruins for the greater part of the day before they were rescued. At that time, Frankland resolved that if he ever got out he would correct all his misdeeds. The next day after his rescue he led Agnes to church, and they became man and wife. In 1756, they were welcomed again to Boston, where he bought, as a town house, the beautiful Clarke mansion, on Garden Court Street, next to Governor Hutchinson's. On the anniversary of the Lisbon earthquake, he would retire to a room of his Hopkinton house and put on the same clothes which he had worn on that day, and keep fast the whole day.

After another visit to Lisbon as consul-general, and again to Boston in 1763, he went to England, where he died in the city of Bath in 1768. The bereaved Agnes returned to Boston and retired to her Hopkinton house, where she was living when Boston was besieged by the republicans in 1775. All her gratitude and affection were locked up by the armed bands of the Continental Congress in Boston. And she was loyal.

In answer to her request that she might move to Boston, the committee of safety wrote her May 15th: "On application of Lady Frankland—voted, that she have liberty to pass into Boston with the following goods and articles for her voyage: 6 trunks, 1 chest, 3 beds and bedding, 6 wethers, 2 pigs, 1 small keg pickled tongues, some hay, 3 bags of corn and such other goods as she thinks proper." The following permit was granted: "To the colony guard—Permit Lady Frankland of Hopkinton, with her attendants, goods and the provisions above mentioned, to pass to Boston. By express order of committee of safety, Benjamin Church, chairman, headquarters, May 15th, 1775."

But the people of Hopkinton, because she was a Royalist, prevented her leaving, stole her goods and abused her attendants, until she brought the matter before Congress. May 18th Congress agreed that: "Lady Frankland be permitted to pass to Boston with the following articles: 7 trunks, all the beds and furniture with them, all boxes and crates, a basket of chickens, a bag of corn, 2 barrels and a hamper, 2 horses and 2 chaises and all the articles in the chaises except arms and ammunition, 1 phaeton, some tongues, ham and veal, sundry small bundles, which are to be examined by a committee of Congress."

May 19th, Col. Bond, with a guard of six men appointed to escort her to Boston, passed her through the lines, where a copy of the congressional resolution was shown. She lived in Boston during the siege at her house on Garden Court Street and departed with the British, March 17th, 1776. She went to Bath, England, where she died in 1783.

CHAPTER V.

Declaration of Independence.

With the continued violation of every constitutional arrangement by the London Parliament going out of its own constituency to invade the constituency of the united provinces, which were fiefs of the Crown, besides independent within themselves, with a state of hostility progressing, a declaration of independence became absolutely necessary. The extreme loyalists held that that declaration should have been against parliament alone and not made to include the King. But the major part of colonials—royalists as well as republicans—agreed that the King, already of an unconstitutional dynasty in Britain, had forfeited all rights to allegiance in America by combining against his own prerogative in the colonies, which the colonists up to this time had maintained for him by force of arms. Therefore, exercising this right, the colonies, by their Congress, on July 4th, 1776, declared their independence.

The extreme loyalists viewed it in this manner: Ryerson's *"Loyalists of America,"* Vol. I., p. 496, says: "The Declaration of Independence was a renunciation of all the principles on which the General Congress, Provincial Legislatures and Conventions professed to act from the beginning of the contest." (p. 499) "It was a violation of good faith to the statesmen and numerous other parties in England, in and out of parliament, who had supported the agents and character of the colonists during the whole contest." (p. 501) "It was also a violation of good faith and justice to their colonial fellow-countrymen who continued to adhere to connection with the mother country on principles professed in all times past by the separatists themselves." (p. 504) "It was the commencement of persecution, proscription and confiscation of property against those who refused to renounce the oath they had taken, and the principles and traditions which, until then, had been acknowledged by their persecutors as well."

As government by "Constitutional" means is inimical to revolutionary methods, the Declaration of Independence from the government and authority of Great Britain rests on the assumption that that government and authority had departed from "Constitutional measures," and had commenced illegitimate and revolutionary action in the colonies, usurping the rights and privileges involved in the colonial charters.

By this declaration infringements of the colonial constitution are held to be sufficient justifications for rebellion, and such infringements are deemed not only tyrannical, but as unconstitutional, they absolve from their allegiance those who adhere to constitutional methods. This absolution from allegiance is a relief granted in that system of law which is the origin of modern law—namely, the Feudal System. It is exercised by the liegeman, the vassal and the grand feudatory whenever their suzerain or feudal superior is lacking in those observances agreed on at the beginning of the feude. In Glasson's *Historie du Droit et des Institution de la France*, the ethics of this system are treated of minutely and historically. The two parts of the contract which exist between the governed and the ruler in feudal law are *fealty* and *mandium*. The *governed* consents to the rulership and plan of government by an oath to maintain it against every foe. The *ruler* promises not to depart from the plan and government to which the *governed* has consented and sworn to maintain. In the feudal law, every man's consent is asked by some feudal superior, and if he be unwilling to be bound by ties of authority to one, he has liberty to turn to another. But after he has once consented by his feud, by his agreement he can be released from it only by a failure on the part of the one to whom he has bound himself by fealty to perform the obligation of the contract.

An illustrious example preserved in English History of this absolution of allegiance on the part of the liegemen, vassals and grand-feudatories towards their feudal superior the king, on account of his failure to perform his mandium, is mentioned in Stubb's *"Constit. Hist. of Eng.,"* Vol. III., p. 380, when Sir William Trussel, proctor of the Lords and Commons, dissolved the kingship of

Edward II. in 1327 with the following words:—"I, William Trussell, proctor of the Prelates, Earls and Barons, and others having full and sufficient power, declare that the hommage and fealty to you, Edward, once King of England, has ceased to exist, and that you are no more King of this realm." Then Sir Thomas Blount, steward of the Household, broke his staff of office in token that his master had ceased to reign. The accusations brought against Edward II. by Stratford were that he "had thrown all the business of state on his favorites, had listened to no complaints against them and had allowed them to commit acts of illegal oppression, which he, himself, had neither the will, nor the energy, to command." But they did not pretend to invade the legitimate prerogative of the Crown or to alter the succession and dynasty.

THE DECLARATION OF AMERICAN INDEPENDENCE commences with an introduction in which it is declared that the reasons for it should be made known. This is just and proper. After which is related some "self-evident truths," which are out of place in a declaration of the reasons or causes, for independence and which belong to theoretical or speculative government.

The *causes* for the Declaration are enumerated finally, many of which are exaggerated, but the principal ones are valid enough to dissolve the allegiance between the colonies and the London government. The colonial charters whose infringements are claimed hereby had been granted by the Stuart Dynasty which had been set aside unconstitutionally in Britain, and the Hanoverian Dynasty being seated on the British throne in place thereof had been adverse to these charters which had been granted by the legitimate House. The *cause in general* for absolution from allegiance is contained in Article 18:—"He has combined with others to subject us to a jurisdiction *foreign to our Constitutions* (i.e., Charters), *and unacknowledged by our laws,* giving his assent to their acts of *pretended* legislation."

The colonial justification is:—*To maintain chartered rights and privileges.* By publishing this justification the support of the major part of the colonials was obtained, a few preferring to abide by their allegiance notwithstanding that they had the right, by a lack of *mandium* of their suzerain to withdraw.

Second Declaration of Independence.

The government of the Continental Congress which was established in this justification, however, from 1776 to 1781, proceeded to exercise the prerogatives of government contrary to the publication which they had made and as subversive of the chartered rights and privileges of the Constitutions of the colonies, as the abuses of authority which had been ascribed to the British government in this publication. The result was another Declaration of Independence on the part of those who adhered to a strict and legal interpretation of the colonial charters. This second Declaration issued by a number of the noblest colonists justifies itself in the following manner for withdrawing support from this congress *which had, in its turn, violated its trust, or mandium.*

The following is an abstract of this "declaration" as it appeared in *Rivington's Royal Gazette,* of New York, November 17th, 1781:—"When in the course of human events it becomes necessary for men, in order to preserve their lives, liberties and properties, and to secure to themselves and to their posterity that peace, liberty and safety are entitled, to throw off and renounce all allegiance to a government which under the insidious pretences of securing those inestimable blessings to them, has wholly deprived them of any security of either life, liberty, property, peace or safety, a decent respect for the opinions of mankind requires that they should declare the injuries and oppressions, the arbitrary and dangerous proceedings which impel them to transfer their allegiance from such, their oppressors, to those who have offered to become their protectors" . . .

"Whenever any form of government becomes destructive to these ends (life, liberty and happiness) it is the right of the people to alter or to abolish it. . . . It is not prudent to change for light and transient causes, . . . but when a long train of the most licentious and despotic abuses . . . evinces a design to reduce them under anarchy and the distractions of democracy

... it is their right, it becomes their duty, to disclaim and renounce all allegiance to such government." ...

"Such have been our patient sufferings, and such is now the necessity which constrains us to renounce all allegiance to Congress, or to the governments lately established by their direction."

The history of Congress is a history of continued weakness, inconsistency, violation of the most sacred obligations of all public faith and honor, and of usurpation —all having in direct object the production of anarchy, civil feuds and violent injustice, which have rendered us miserable, and must soon establish tyranny over us and our country."

"To prove this let parts be submitted to the candid world:"

* * * * * *

II. "Availing themselves of our zeal and unanimity to oppose the claims of the British Parliament, and of our unsuspecting confidence in their solemn professions and declarations, they have forbidden us to listen to, or accept, any terms of peace until their assent should be obtained."

III. "They have refused to accept of, or even to receive, proposals and terms of accommodation, though they know the terms offered exceeded what the colonies in America had unanimously declared would be satisfactory unless the crown would relinquish a right inestimable to it and to the whole empire, and formidable to Congress only."

IV. "They have excited and directed the people to alter or annul their ancient constitutions, under which they and their ancestors had been happy for many ages, for the sole purpose of promoting their measures."

V. "They have by mobs and riots awed representative houses into compliance with their resolutions, though destructive of the peace, liberty and safety of the people."

* * * * * *

VIII. "They have corrupted all the sources of justice and equity by this Tender Law, by which they destroyed the legal force of all civil contracts, wronged the honest creditor and deserving salary man of his just dues, stripped the helpless orphan of his patrimony, and the disconsolate widow of her dower."

* * * * * *

XII. "They have ruined our trade and destroyed our credit with all parts of the world."

XIII. "They have forced us to receive their paper for goods, merchandise and for money due us, equal to silver and gold, and then by a breach of public faith in not redeeming the same, and by the most infamous bankruptcy, have left it on our hands to the total ruin of multitudes and to the injury of all."

XIV. "They have driven many of our people beyond sea into exile, and have confiscated their estates and the estates of others who were beyond sea before the war, or the existence of Congress, on pretence of offenses and under the sanction of mock trial to which the person condemned was neither cited nor present."

XV. "They have abolished the true system of the English Constitution and laws in 13 of the American provinces, and have established therein a weak and factious democracy, and have attempted to use them as introducing the same misrule and disorder into all the colonies on the continent."

XVI. "They have recommended the abolition of our charters." . . .

XVII. "They have destroyed all good order and government by plunging us in the factions of democracy." . . .

* * * * * *

XIX. "They have, without consent and knowledge of the legislature, invited over an army of foreign mercenaries to support them and their faction." . . .

XX. "They have fined, imprisoned, banished and put to death some of our fellow-citizens for no other cause but attachment to the (ancient) laws and constitution."

* * * * * *

XXII. "They first attempted to gain the savage and merciless Indians to their side, but failing in making them the presents promised and expected, have occasioned an indistinguishable destruction to ages, sexes and conditions on our frontiers."

XXIV. "They have wantonly violated our public faith . . . and have not blushed to act in direct contradiction to their most solemn declarations."

XXV. . . . "The unsuspecting confidence which we, with our fellow-citizens, reposed in the Congress of 1774; the unanimous applause with which their patriotism and firmness were crowned for having stood forth as the champions of our rights, founded on the English Constitution; at the same time while it gave to Congress the unanimous support of the whole continent, inspired their successors with very different ideas, and emboldened them by degrees to pass measures directly the reverse of those before adopted." . . . "Congress in 1774, reprobated every idea of separation from Great Britain. . . . They declared that the repeal of certain acts would restore our ancient peace and harmony; that they asked but for peace, liberty and safety; that they wished not for a diminution of the royal prerogative. And they pledged themselves in the presence of Almighty God that they will ever carefully and zealously endeavor to support and maintain the royal authority."

XXVI. "The acts complained of have been repealed, yet how have Congress given the lie to these their most solemn professions!" . . . "We find them contending for liberty of speech, and at the same time controlling the press by means of a mob, and persecuting everyone who ventures to hint his disapprobation of their proceedings."

XXVII. "We find them declaring in September, 1779, that to pay off their paper money at less than its nominal value would be an unpardonable sin, an execrable deed; that a faithless bankrupt republic would be a novelty in the political world, and appear like a common prostitute among chaste and reputable matrons; would be 'a reproach and a byword among the nations,' etc. We find the same Congress in March liquidating their paper debt at 2½ per cent., or sixpence in the pound."

* * * * * *

XXVIII. "We have sufficiently shown that a government thus marked and distinguished from every other . . . by the enormity of its excesses and infamy is unfit to rule a free people."

XXIX. "We, therefore, natives and citizens of America, appealing to the impartial world to judge of the justice of our cause, but above all to the Supreme Judge of the world for the rectitude of our intentions, do renounce and disclaim all allegiance, duty or submission to the Congress, or to any government under them, and declare that the United Colonies, or States so-called, neither are, nor of right ought to be independent of the crown of Great Britain, or unconnected with that empire . . . and in the support of this declaration with a firm reliance on the support of Divine Providence, we mutually pledge to each other and to the Crown and Empire . . . our lives, our fortunes and our sacred honour."

This Second Declaration of Independence, this time from the "Continental Congress," needs no comment as the publication of the first is the justification of the second.

That the Continental Congress in which a radical majority had overruled the voice of a wise minority was unconstitutional may be seen by reading the Articles of the *"Minute Men,"* which organization supplied the real force of resistance to the unconstitutional procedure of the English Parliament in the colonies. These Articles are:—

Articles of the Minute Men.

I. "To defend to the utmost of our power His Majesty King George III., his person, crown and dignity."

II. "At the same time to the utmost of our power and ability to defend all of our chartered rights, liberties and privileges."

III. "And at all times and in all places to obey our officers, chosen by us, and our superior officers, in ordering and disciplining us when and where said officers shall think proper,"

The King a Factor of the Charters.

It may be seen by these Articles that the only unconstitutional acts complained of were those acts of the English Parliament which infringed the chartered rights of the colonies. The Colonial Charters acknowledged the King as their suzerain and the Continental Congress had sworn to maintain the rights of the Colonial Charters. This oath was their *mandium* to the colonists in fulfillment of which only could they expect their allegiance.

CHAPTER VI.

The Climax.

After the British troops had retired from Boston they took possession of New York City, which they determined to retain as an army-depot and place for reserves. Washington's army followed them from Dorchester, and on Long Island, Aug. 27th, 1776, felt strong enough to face the troops of Clinton, Grant and de Heister in open fight. After a short engagement, the Colonists were defeated and fled in the greatest confusion, leaving 1,000 dead on the field and a large number as prisoners. Among these were Lord Sterling and Gen. Sullivan.

Lord Howe paroled Gen. Sullivan and sent him with a message to Congress, that he would confer with some of its members as private citizens, in regard to a settlement of the difficulty between them and parliament. He and his brother, Gen. Howe, had been empowered by the home-government to compromise this dispute, if possible.

Congress authorized Dr. Franklin, John Adams and Edward Rutledge to act officially. In the conference which followed, Lord Howe declared that he could go no further than to "grant pardons on their submission to British rule." But the Colonists were not fighting for pardons and they refused to abandon their position. They knew that France, Spain and Holland were about to take part in the struggle and they felt that these powers would gain for them their independence and that they would have the plunder of the loyalists besides.

At this, the British in full possession of New York, matured a plan to push forward advance-posts into the interior, capture Philadelphia and drive Washington's army and Congress into the Southern provinces. Then keeping this line a trocha from New York to Philadelphia, to extend another line up the Hudson River and meet Gen. Burgoigne's army that had begun its march from Canada down the Lake Champlain district. To

The Climax.

resist this the Colonists had strong entrenchments on the Hudson and a good army under Gen. Gates to confront Burgoigne.

Gen. Sir William Howe with the British troops entered Philadelphia in triumph Sept. 26th, 1777, and another British expedition captured Forts Montgomery and Clinton on the Hudson (Oct. 6th.) But Oct. 7th, Gen. Burgoigne was unable to force his way through Gates' army in the Battles of Stillwater, where he was overthrown by the incomparable valor of the Scottish Colonial regiments of New Hampshire and Kentucky, under Starke and Morgan. In spite of this triumph, the Colonists would have been broken speedily had not aid arrived from the outside. Washington's army was fugitive, starving and deserting at Valley Forge, when France and Spain began to send troops, arms and ships of war for the expulsion of the British from the continent.

In 1779 Washington wrote: "France by her supplies has saved us from the yoke thus far. . . . The recruits of 1780 could not have been armed without the 50 tons of ammunition supplied by the French."

On receipt of the news of Burgoigne's defeat and of the declaration of war by France and Spain, which nations had recognized the legitimate position of the united provinces, consternation prevailed in England. Immediately bills were passed in the British Parliament (1778) granting all that the colonists had demanded. But Congress rejected all overtures,—France having acknowledged the independence of the United States.

In September, the same year, a Scot, Capt. John Paul Jones, in command of a French frigate, but with a commission from the colonies, met the British man-of-war "Sarapis," and captured her after a most desperate fight, his ship, the "Bonhomme Richard," going down in the conflict.

Lord Cornwallis, the British commander in the South, after he had gained successes over Gen. Greene and had routed completely Gen. Gates, of whom it was said that he had "exchanged Northern laurel for Southern cypress," had taken up quarters in Yorktown. There, in that port, whose excellent harbor offered easy access to the sea, he awaited reënforcements from the British reserves at New York, Rochambeau, commanding the French army in America, was informed of this, and he suggested to Washington the plan for the capture of the British general. In combination with the French fleet of the Count de Grasse, which blocked the entrance to the harbor, the land forces shut in Cornwallis by a sudden move and he was obliged to surrender after an ineffectual attempt to cut his way out.

This surrender, of Oct. 19th, 1781, showed the British the folly of continuing the combat, for in April of the next year, Holland joined her arms against Britain and Russia united with Denmark in an armed neutrality. News arrived at the same time that Hyder Allee had invaded British India at the head of 200,000 men. Then Britain decided to abandon the war in America to confront dangers which were menacing her own shores. During this war the most loyal province was Georgia. She was the last to send delegates to the Continental Congress. The Georgia royalists organized a separate government in 1778 and in 1779 made a separate treaty with the Crown. As a military order, they held the colony free from republican domination until 1782. Even then they promised to expell all revolutionists and republicans and to preserve the province under the protection of the British Empire if but one British regiment might be added to their own Georgia Rangers.

In South Carolina and Virginia the attachment to the Crown had not been quenched even after the imposition of the new republican model in 1787. In South Carolina during this war there were manifested the greatest animosities between the two parties. Here were perpetrated the greatest atrocities in a warfare of mutual extermination. Yet after the triumph of the revolutionary faction in 1783, no colonial legislature dealt so leniently with the unfortunate royalist families who remained. And this was because, in the Southern colonies, the entire population had been more favorable to a royal form of government.

In the North, on the other hand, the meanest persecution that only the basest Yankee mind could conceive

The Climax. 107

was heaped on those royalists who remained—but there were very few who were so stupid as to offer themselves a sacrifice for the gratification of the cruelty of the democrats. In this war for American independence, from first to last, on the independence side, there had been in the field 396,286 troops. This enumeration includes the continentals, the regulars and the state militia. Outside of these, there were small partizan corps whose numbers cannot be ascertained. Sabine, in his *"American Loyalists,"* estimates the number of loyalists in the British army at one time as high as 20,000. This war had been terminated by the preliminaries of a negotiation for peace which were signed by the representatives of Great Britain and the United States, secretly, at Paris, November, 1782. Although the Yankees had pledged to the French King an alliance in exchange for his aid, not to be broken without his consent, yet when the British ambassador approached the Yankee commissioners at Paris and offered great inducements for them to betray their trust, they concluded this arrangement unknown to the French court. It was the beginning of the illustration of those peculiarities of Yankee diplomacy in history which have ceased to be the wonder of nations.

April 11th, 1783, peace was proclaimed by Congress. The 19th it was announced by Washington to the army. Sept. 3rd, France, Spain, and Holland had concluded their treaty of pacification. Nov. 23rd, the British fleet sailed from New York, which had been held ever since the Battle of Long Island in 1776.

The American colonies which were named by Britain as "free, sovereign and independent states" were acknowledged each as a nation. The royal charter of each was its constitution of government. But the revolutionists very soon turned on the royalists who remained in the colonies and destroyed every vestige of these charters in a government of universal sufferage, rapine and plunder, which was not fully extended until after the civil war of 1861-5 had reduced the Southern provinces to the same illegal and majority-ridden régime. As for these Yankee democrats, on account of their greed, theft and lack of honor, their French allies "held them in the greatest contempt for their venality and baseness."

Washington wrote, Dec. 30th, 1778: "Speculation, peculation and an insatiable thirst for riches seem to have got the better of every consideration and almost of every order of men." July 10th, 1782: "That spirit of freedom, which at the commencement of the contest would have gladly sacrificed everything to the attainment of the object, has long since subsided and every selfish passion, has taken its place." La Fayette wrote to Washington, June 12th, 1779: "For God's sake prevent Congress from disputing so loudly together. Nothing so much hurts the interests and reputation of America."

Most of their motives were contemptible, although hidden beneath plausible pretexts. In Sabine's *"American Loyalists,"* Vol. I., p. 56, it is written: "Otis was revengeful because the Crown did not make his father a judge in Massachusetts. John Adams became a rebel because he was refused a commission as Justice of the Peace; Sam. Adams, because he had been dismissed as a defaulting collector of taxes; Hancock, to escape paying smuggling fines and on account of wounded vanity. Joseph Warren was a broken man and sought speculating in civil strife to better his condition. Washington was soured because he had not been retained in the British army for his services during the French and Indian wars. The Lees were all unsound men, and Richard Henry Lee was disappointed in not receiving the office of stamp distributor which he had solicited, and Franklin at the opposition to his land scheme and plan for settlement on the Ohio."

These people, after coming into supreme control, turned against the aristocracy remaining in the colonies —even those members who had been dupes of their promises and had proffered aid. They repudiated all the indebtedness of the government to its own citizens, so that Robert Morris, who had pledged his fortune to the cause, died in a debtor's prison; Governor Langdon of New Hampshire with scores of others were reduced to poverty; Gen. George Rogers Clarke, who had conquered the West, was in such miserable poverty that he entered the military services of a foreign prince; John Paul, alias Jones, the ablest sea-captain and the founder of their navy, followed after Clarke, and a nephew of Washington died with the rank of Colonel in the armies of Greece, cursing his country. The few families of eminence that survived the insidious machinations of Congress against the aristocracy owed their survival to territorial grants they had held from the Crown in the colonies—for all those who had pledged their property in defense of the new states were robbed by their government, in the repudiation of all indebtedness towards its defenders.

Not only this, but they proceeded gradually to alter, abridge or modify the charters which they had claimed to defend, or else interpret their meaning in such a way as to destroy their significance in every state. The revolutionary government of France, which was modeled closely after the one set up in America, proceeded along the same lines, and, as Glasson says, "destroyed the feudality and the obligations subsisting between it and the people. From that time there was no pact, or contract, between the government and the people, as formerly, only the will of a majority composed of ignorant and irresponsible multitudes."

The English government itself, at the close of this war, when making the Treaty of Peace of 1783 with the American commissioners at Paris, out of revenge, most likely against the royalists for their first opposition to the London Parliament, insisted on no terms to prevent their suffering from further depredations in America. Ryerson (Vol. II., p. 164-5) says on this subject: "A campaign for the purpose, on the refusal of the American commissioners to recognize what was sanctioned by the laws and usages of nations, would have been honorable to the British government and popular in England. . . England was mistress of the seas, held New York, Charleston, Rhode Island, Penobscot and other military ports and could soon have reduced the Americans to do what their peace-commissioners at Paris had refused to do—place British subjects in America on the same footing as to property that they possessed before the war. . . England could have easily and successfully refused granting the United States one foot of land beyond the limits of the 13 colonies and thus have secured those vast Western territories, now the larger part of the United

States, and retained her garrisons in New York, Rhode Island and Charleston to hold those places as guarantees until the performance of these requisitions on the part of the United States."

But the people in control in England ever since the Revolution of 1688 dethroned the Aryan aristocracy have degenerated slowly in the grander traits of rulership. Suported by the wealth of a colossal empire whose forward movement has not yet lost its momentum, although relaxed in vital energy by this displacing of classes, the power of England seems to be greater by this inflation. But as Tyndal says in his *"Life of the Earl of Strafford"*: "It remains to be seen whether the many (the Anglo-Saxon democracy) can retain what the few (the Franco-Norman, or Gothic, aristocracy) have won." They have commenced by losing the richest empire in America the world has ever seen.

PART V.—CHAPTER I.

Confederation of the Royalist Orders for Constitutional Recognition.

I.

"Let our halls and towers decay,
  Be our name and line forgot,
Lands and manours pass away,—
  We but share our Monarch's lot.
If no more our annals show
  Battles won and banners taken,
Still in death, defeat and woe,
  Ours be loyalty unshaken!"

II.

"Constant still in danger's hour,
  Princes own'd our fathers' aid;
Lands and honors, wealth and power
  Well this loyalty repaid.
Perish wealth and power and pride!
  Mortal boons by mortals given;
But let Constancy abide,—
  Constancy, the gift of Heaven."

(Rokeby by Sir Walter Scott.)

The cardinal principles of the Royalists as United Empire Loyalists are included in the three articles of the Minute Men, viz.: I. To defend the Royal Prerogative and Honor and Dignity of the Crown in the Colonies. II. To defend the Constitution of the Provinces against any infringements by the London Parliament, or the Colonial Democracy. III. To combine together for these purposes, and choose their leaders and obey them. These Minute Men fought against the pretensions of the London Parliament in America until 1778 when that parliament rescinded all its acts of interference with the royal prerogative in the colonies and with the provisions of the

Colonial Charters, or Constitutions. Then the Minute Men disbanded and demanded a settlement of the matter from Congress, that they had supported until this. But Congress, whose good material had left it in disgust, representing but the riff-raff and democracy refused, and the greater number of the Minute Men, reorganized as Loyalists, turned their arms against those who had perjured their trust and forsaken their allegiance, while others of the Minute Men retired into private life—especially those of the Stuart adherents who were not disposed to go so far as the others for the sake of the usurping House of Hanover.

In 1778 (Feb.) Sir Henry Clinton with authority from the king to recognize the United Empire Loyalists, issued a royal commission for such purpose to form a council for the "Associated Loyalists of America" to William Franklin, Governor of New Jersey; J. S. Martin, Governor of North Carolina; Gen. Timothy Ruggles, and Hons. Daniel Coxe, G. Ludlow, Edward Lutwyche, George Romer, George Leonard, Anthony Stewart and Robert Alexander.

The Presidents of the various colonial branches in 1779, given in Ryerson, Vol. II., p. 182 (Loyalists of America"), were: Sir William Pepperrell, Massachusetts; Sir John Wentworth, New Hampshire; Hon. George Rowe, Rhode Island; Gen. James de Lancey, New York; Hon. David Ogden, New Jersey; Hon. Joseph Galloway, Pennsylvania and Deleware; Hon. Robert Alexander, Maryland; Maj. James R. Grymes, Virginia; Hon. Henry Eustace McCulloch, North Carolina; Atty, Gen. James Simpson, South Carolina; Hon. William Knox and Lieut.-Gov. John Graham, Georgia. The regiments raised and officered by them were The King's Rangers, The Royal Fencible-Americans, New York Volunteers, King's American Regiment, Prince of Wales' American Volunteers, Maryland Loyalist Regiment, De Lancey's Battalion, 2nd American Regiment, King's Carolina Rangers, South Carolina Royal Regt., North Carolina Highland Regt., King's American Dragoons, Loyal American Regt., American Legion, New Jersey Volunteers, British Legion, Loyal Forresters,

Confederation of the Royalist Orders. 113

Orange Rangers, Pennsylvania Loyal Regt., Guides and Pioneers, North Carolina Volunteers, Georgia's Loyal Rangers, West Chester Volunteers, Loyal New Englanders, Associated Loyalist Militia, New Hampshire Loyalists, Hamilton's New York Battalions.

For Canada there were raised by the Loyalists (French and Scotch) two regiments of their Seigneurial Guard; the first, under the Colonel, Baron de Longueuil, was directed to the relief of Fort St. Jean-Iberville, the second, sometimes known as the Royal Immigrant Regiment, commanded by those Scottish Seigneurs—former officers of the old 79th Cameronian Highlanders—who had had seigneuries conceded to them by Governor Murray after 1763—assisted Governor Sir Guy Carleton in the successful defence of Quebec.

The two greatest exploits of arms of the Loyalists—apart from those of the regular troops in the field—were the defense of Savannah and the defence of Fort St. Jean.

The Loyalists organized their military order and their rangers in Savannah, Georgia, in 1778, under command of Gen. John Prevost, who came up from St. Augustine in Florida for the purpose. The next year, the royal governor, Sir James Wright, baronet, returned from England and took supreme command. Gen. Lincoln, commanding the republican force in the vicinity, determined to capture Savannah, the royalist stronghold, and combined his movements with a great French fleet under the Comte d'Estang, which carried also an army of the veteran troops of France. In the attack which followed, the heavy cannon of the French, swept the ramparts of Savannah and silenced all the cannon of the royalists. Then the French and republican troops were massed and advanced to carry the intrenchments by the bayonet, as the royalists refused to surrender. But the royalists feared not, they grasped their muskets and sabres with stout hearts and iron hands, stood to the shock and beat back the numerous foe, so that the French were glad to return to their fleet and the republicans to their quarters in Carolina. From that success, the royalists advanced and obtained possession of all of Georgia as far North as Augusta, and held the province until the treaty of peace of 1783 delivered it over to the enemy, in spite of their protests of possession.

The most important action, from its effect of preserving Canada to the crown, was the defense of Fort St. Jean, Sept. 5th, 1775; the American Generals, Montgomery and Schuyler, with 2,000 men, appeared before Fort St. Jean, on their way to capture Montreal, Three Rivers and Quebec. The English of the lower class in the country encouraged the insurgents; the French of the lower class were inclined the same way and were prevented going over to the enemy in a body only by the priests, who feared for their own rights under a revolutionary and puritanical regime. The seigneurs and officers of the noblesse, both French, and Scottish, the latter of whom had received seigneurial grants from Governor Murray, raised a seigneurial guard of two contingents, one of which, mostly Scottish, was directed towards Quebec, the other, mostly French, under the Baron de Longueuil, was sent to relieve Fort St. Jean. The arrival of this little company of *élite* at the fort raised the spirits of the garrison, whose officers were induced thereby to make a vigorous defense. This Seigneurial Guard did most of the fighting during the 45 days of resistance which held the American army back among the marshes of the Richelieu. It was among them only that any were killed in sortis. And when by lack of succor, and of provisions, the place surrendered finally, the delay had enabled Sir Guy Carleton to put Quebec in such a condition of defense that it held the disaffected in the country quiet and beat off the last efforts of the foe. From this time and until after the conclusion of the peace of 1783 Canada became the objective point of settlement for the 45,000 American loyalists who were directed towards Canada by land and sea with their wives and children and such poor relics of their former affluance, which they could carry with them from the clutches of an insolvent and cruel foe. Towns sprang up in the old province where they settled; the new provinces of New Brunswick (1784) and Ontario (1791) were created by them; refinement, wealth, and above all loyalty to principle—the best heritage—followed in their footsteps. They and the French royalists "have proved a barrier to the growth of any annexation party" (Bourinot, *"Story of Canada,"* p. 292). "Although no noble monument has been raised to these founders of new provinces . . . yet the names of all are written in imperishable letters in provincial annals . . . and one who traces to this source is as proud of his lineage as a Derby or a Talbot of Malahide, or an inheritor of other noble name" (ibid, pp. 296-7). "They were an army of leaders, for it was the loftiest heads that attracted the hate of the revolutionists. The most influential judges, distinguished lawyers, capable and prominent physicians, most highly educated of the clergy, the royal councillors of the colonies, crown officers, people of culture and social distinction" (Roberts' *"Hist. of Canada,"* p. 202). "They were the gentry (noblesse) of the American colonies" (Lecky, *"Hist. of England"*).

As a gentry, a noblesse, they were incorporated in Canada with the constitution and principles for which they had fought and which the crown and parliament had guaranteed, as well as by Act of the Sovereign Council of Quebec, Nov. 9th, 1789, to wit:—"In presence of the Governor, Lord Dorchester, and Royal Councillors, the Hons. William Smith, Hugh Finlay, Thomas Dunn, J. G. Chossegros de Léry, F. Baby, Charles de Lanaudière, Lecompte Dupré, etc., his Lordship intimated to the council that it was his wish to put a Mark of Honor on the families that had adhered to the unity of the Empire and had joined the Royal Standard in America before the Treaty of Separation of 1783" . . . "The Council concurred and it was ordered that the several Land Boards take course for preserving a Registry of all persons falling under description aforesaid so that their posterity may be distinguished from other settlers." . . They were entitled to write the letters "U.E." (United Empire) after their names as an inheritance of distinction to their posterity in the family name of the original loyalists and as a means of taking precedence of others of the same rank —an U. E. Seigneur, before a seigneur; an U. E. gentleman, before a gentleman.

Besides this creation by law of a precedence for the Order of the United Empire, the agreement of the British government that the constitution of Canada by the Act of 1774 should not be altered and by the Act of 1778 that the meaning of the Anglo-American constitution should not be infringed, recognized virtually the right of representation in the council of the province of the colonial aristocracy; it confirmed the laudable practise on the part of the governor of keeping a registry for the colony and the king of the best families for appointment in the council. The Lords of Manours and Patroons in New York, the Lords of Manours in Maryland, the Landgraves and Caciques in Carolina, the European noblesse and chivalry established in landed tenure in the other colonies and in Florida, the relics of the aristocracy deriving from the Order of the Empire of Charles V., whose first creation in America was the duchy of Veragua in Central America to the grandson of Christopher Columbus from this time saw their hopes realized in Canada.

In framing the model of government for Canada in 1791, based on this constitution—any model is null not so based—Lord William Pitt prepared for the honest practise which all colonial charters demanded, and which the Houses of Lords and Commons acknowledged anew in passing the bill. This bill provided for sittings in the Upper House in Canada to be annexed to hereditary honors in the colony. But the ministry in England and the governors sent over from England made no effort to put this acknowledgement in practise, and the politicians of Canada, ever fearful of the aristocracy, worked to oppose it and to ostracise and keep from public position the descendants of the patricians and founders of the country. In 1879 the descendants of these various orders of nobility, knighthood and chivalry in the old colonies (United States and Canada) took up the movement of their organization—although a movement had been suggested as early as 1798. The old order of the Empire of Charles V. in America was reorganized under the name of the Aryan Order of the Empire and reserved for the descendants of the Royalists of 1776-83, known as the Order of the United Empire, the Seigneurs of Canada, the Baronets of Nova Scotia, the Patrons and Lords of Manors of New York and Maryland, the Landgraves and Caciques of Carolina, and other patrician families established on landed tenure in America. It was decided that "none but those of the White Aryan race shall be elegible, notwithstanding what their other claims may be." The first chancellor of the order in 1879 was the late Frederic Forsyth, Viscount de Fronsac, succeeded by Gen. Alex. P. Stewart of Mississippi, and he by Gen. John B. Gordon, of Georgia, and he by Sir Edward Warren, of Paris, and he by Harvey Leonadas Byrd, M.D., President of the Baltimore Medical College and a descendant of the renowned Sir William Byrd of Westover, Virginia. It counted among the early members Dr. Olando Fairfax, Richmond, Virginia; Dr. Leprohon, of Montreal, French Consul at Portland, Maine; Thomas Supplee, of Ohio; W. L. Ritter, of Baltimore, etc., until in 1891 the Chancellorship fell to Dr. Joseph Gaston Bulloch, of Savannah, Georgia, who published a pamphlet on the order the next year. In 1894 the State of Georgia granted the council the privilege of incorporation.

But the order was attacked by the republican press throughout the United States; it was accused of desiring to restore an empire, and of organizing an aristocracy on the principle that "a good name is rather to be chosen than great riches"; it was condemned for recognizing the truths of history and the laws of Nature. It became impossible for its continuance in the United States, where the edicts of majority-rule have declared that the lowest man who votes, whether negro or white, is the standard of selection and that there shall be no other standard of race recognized above this equality; it had gathered together the widely scattered of the legitimist families from the obscurity of their private life and endowed them with a corporate existence. Already the proper place, where these various orders of the colonies have a legal and constitutional recognition, was made manifest by those of the United Empire Loyalists in St. John, New Brunswick, forming a branch society in 1883 under the presidency of Sir Leonard Tilley, lieutenant-governor of the province, who was succeeded later by Sir John C. Allen, the chief-justice. In 1896, on a large scale, Frederic Gregory Forsyth, Viscount de Fronsac at Montreal, on May 18th, with a brief from the Aryan Order, laid the foundation of the United Empire Loyalist Association of Canada and was succeeded in the presidency of the general body by Sir William Johnson, Baronet of Chambly,

grandson of the great Sir John Johnson, Baronet, who
led his battalions of loyalist troops into Canada in 1783.
The next year (1896), by letters from the Viscount de
Fronsac to Col. W. Hamilton Merritt of Toronto, a division was established there under presidency of the Hon.
John Beverley Robinson, lieutenant-governor of Ontario,
and grandson of the U. E. Loyalist, Lieutenant-Governor
Sir Frederic Phillippse Robinson, baronet, who came to
Ontario in 1783. In 1897 by the energy of Rev. Arthur
Pyke, member of the general council at Montreal, the
Nova Scotia division was established at Halifax under
presidency of the Hon. A. G. Jones, now (1905) lieutenant-governor of Nova Scotia. About the same time the
descendants of the Seigneurs of Canada in the Aryan Order chose as their president Charles Coleman Grant,
Baron de Longueuil, replaced at his death by his
brother. Reginald d' Iberville Grant, Baron de
Longueuil. There remains yet in the Aryan Order
for choice of officers under its own ancient charter, the
descendants of the Baronets of Nova Scotia. The movement of reorganization although participated in by Canadian descendants had taken place first in the United
States, because, strange as it may seem, there were individuals there stronger and more independent in royalist
belief and sentiment, at that time (1879-80) than in Canada. They were the relics few and far between—but
mostly in the Southern States,—of those Royalist and
Cavalier families who had fought for the Stuarts under
Charles I. and James II., and had been the "first to charge
the foe, on Preston's bloody sod" in the time of Prince
Charlie (1745). They were of the Royalist Minute-men
of 1776-8, who, while guarding the prerogative of the
crown in the colonial charter, refused to recognize the
Hanoverian usurpation outside of those charters, and had
gone to their homes in 1778 rather than fight against the
colonies with the U. E. Loyalists, after the charters were
assured. They had spurned with contempt the supercilious condescension of the court of George III. that was
offering them "pardons" if they submitted to its insolent
and illegal domination in the colonies. But they were
royalists and turned with even greater scorn from the
dishonest propaganda of the Yankee republic. As Pol-

lard in his *"Lost Cause"* says, "There could be no congeniality between the Puritan exiles who sought the cheerless shores of New England and the cavaliers who drank confusion to round-heads and regicides in their baronial halls of Virginia and the Carolinas."

But the foundation for the Order itself in the United States had been destroyed by the overthrow of the colonial charters in the republic. It had a right of existence and of representation however in Canada as a constitutional quantity. By the constitution on which the Dominion of Canada is founded, acknowledged by the capitulations of Montreal of 1760, by the order of creation of the Baronets of Nova Scotia, by the Quebec Act of 1774, by the Acts of Parliament in recognition of similar sovereignty of the colonial constitutions of 1778 (which contained the representation of colonial aristocracy), by the Loyalist Act in 1789—acts in themselves recognizing the irrefragibility of the constitution of the country and which no Canadian, or other parliament, has authority to undo, not even by a "British North American Act," which is null, wherein it disagrees with the above pledges, and when enforced in an unconstitutional manner, absolves from allegiance the same as in 1776 a similar proceeding did. Through the officers the order opened communications with the British and Canadian governments. Dr. Stirling Ryerson, President of the U. E. Loyalist Division at Toronto, was deputed by the other U. E. Loyalist divisions to attend the Queen's Jubilee of 1897 as a representative and to present the address of the various bodies. In that address was a request that the decoration of the Loyalists, designed by Dr. Ryerson, and consisting of a bronze cross of the Victoria pattern, might be recorded with the precedence due it according to the law of 1789. He was referred to the Colonial Secretary, Mr. Chamberlain. To escape the dilemma of a refusal, Mr. Chamberlain said that it would be considered if recommended by the Canadian government. But the Canadian government, in the name of the King, in 1789 had already agreed to the recognition. However, Dr. Ryerson called to see the polite, political and liberal Premier, Laurier, and he with sauve diplomacy postponed action on the matter until a "more propitious season."

During the administration of Lord Aberdeen, the Herald-Marshal, in the name of the Seigneurs of Canada, opened communication with that individual to know what arrangements had been made at the receptions at Ottawa, for the seigneurial precedence. Aberdeen did not deign a reply until he was rudely awakened by a command from his superior, the colonial secretary, to answer the demand of the Seigneurial Order. Then he replied stating that he had "referred the matter to the Canadian government." Absurd,—to a set of politicians who exist solely as a franchise under a constitution, a part of which is the Seigneurial Order itself! Lord Minto, (who had united with these republican politicians and others of that ilk to insult the King's commander in Canada, Lord Dundonald, by signing his dismissal because he had done his duty contrary to the wishes of these politicians) seemed to be ignorant that there was anything in Canada but Himself and Them. But in the meantime the Aryan Order of the Empire in all its branches, perfecting its organization, founded on the constitution, supported by the legitimate prerogative of the crown, and by the vast majority of all the people of the Province of Quebec—who stand by the exact interpretation of the same constitution because it guarantees their religion, law, and language in exchange for their alegiance—is forming a physical force to employ in maintenance of its legal rights. And these rights, in this constitution, by the full strength of the Crown and Majesty of the Empire, by the very oath and mandium of the Sovereign, are bound to be sustained.

INDEX.

	Page.
Introduction	3

PART I.

Chapter I. Colonies under the Stuarts 5
Chapter II. Virginia's Constitutional right exercised of refusing to recognize the English Parliament's participation in Royal Perogative—External dissensions .. 14
Bacon Rebellion of 1676.. 17

PART II.

Chapter I. Maryland, Carolina, New York. The Maryland Lords of Manours 23
Chapter II. The South,—Carolina 35
New York 37
Middle Colonies 43

PART III.

Chapter I. New England Colony and government; founding of Plymouth and Massachusetts Bay Colonies 44
Chapter II. Beginning of Royalists in New England. King's Chapel. The Royal Charter.. 53

PART IV.

UNION ERA.

Chapter I. Parliament usurps Crown functions in the Provinces.. 60
Chapter II. Consolidation on Continental Basis against Parliament usurpation. Parties in the Colonies.. 67
Chapter III. Conspiracy and Hypocracy and Loyalty and Honor armed together 77
Chapter IV. Struggles in the Field 83
Chapter V. Declaration of Independence.. 95
Second Declaration of Independence 98
Articles of Minute-Men 102
King a factor of the Charters 103
Chapter VI. The Climax 104

PART V.

Chapter I. Confederation of the Royalist Orders for Constitutional Recognition 111

Trieste

Trieste Publishing has a massive catalogue of classic book titles. Our aim is to provide readers with the highest quality reproductions of fiction and non-fiction literature that has stood the test of time. The many thousands of books in our collection have been sourced from libraries and private collections around the world.

The titles that Trieste Publishing has chosen to be part of the collection have been scanned to simulate the original. Our readers see the books the same way that their first readers did decades or a hundred or more years ago. Books from that period are often spoiled by imperfections that did not exist in the original. Imperfections could be in the form of blurred text, photographs, or missing pages. It is highly unlikely that this would occur with one of our books. Our extensive quality control ensures that the readers of Trieste Publishing's books will be delighted with their purchase. Our staff has thoroughly reviewed every page of all the books in the collection, repairing, or if necessary, rejecting titles that are not of the highest quality. This process ensures that the reader of one of Trieste Publishing's titles receives a volume that faithfully reproduces the original, and to the maximum degree possible, gives them the experience of owning the original work.

We pride ourselves on not only creating a pathway to an extensive reservoir of books of the finest quality, but also providing value to every one of our readers. Generally, Trieste books are purchased singly - on demand, however they may also be purchased in bulk. Readers interested in bulk purchases are invited to contact us directly to enquire about our tailored bulk rates. Email: customerservice@triestepublishing.com

You May Also Like

Department of the Interior. Miscellaneous Publications, No. 9. Descriptive Catalogue of Photographs of North American Indians

W. H. Jackson

ISBN: 9780649561209
Paperback: 148 pages
Dimensions: 6.14 x 0.32 x 9.21 inches
Language: eng

Church Stories

J. Erskine Clarke

ISBN: 9781760579777
Paperback: 154 pages
Dimensions: 6.14 x 0.33 x 9.21 inches
Language: eng

www.triestepublishing.com

You May Also Like

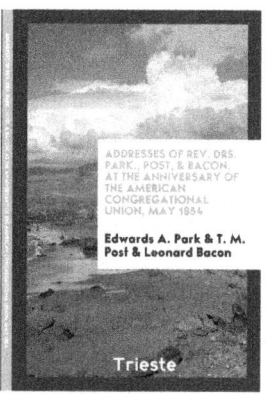

Addresses of Rev. Drs. Park., Post, & Bacon, at the Anniversary of the American Congregational Union, May 1854

Edwards A. Park & T. M. Post & Leonard Bacon

ISBN: 9780649037339
Paperback: 154 pages
Dimensions: 6.14 x 0.33 x 9.21 inches
Language: eng

A Respiration Calorimeter with Appliances for the Direct Determination of Oxygen

W. O. Atwater & F. G. Benedict

ISBN: 9781760576257
Paperback: 248 pages
Dimensions: 6.14 x 0.52 x 9.21 inches
Language: eng

www.triestepublishing.com

You May Also Like

Report of the Department of Farms and Markets, pp. 5-71

Various

ISBN: 9780649333158
Paperback: 84 pages
Dimensions: 6.14 x 0.17 x 9.21 inches
Language: eng

Catalogue of the Episcopal Theological School in Cambridge Massachusetts, 1891-1892

Various

ISBN: 9780649324132
Paperback: 78 pages
Dimensions: 6.14 x 0.16 x 9.21 inches
Language: eng

www.triestepublishing.com

You May Also Like

Three Hundred Tested Recipes

Various

ISBN: 9780649352142
Paperback: 88 pages
Dimensions: 6.14 x 0.18 x 9.21 inches
Language: eng

A Basket of Fragments

Anonymous

ISBN: 9780649419418
Paperback: 108 pages
Dimensions: 6.14 x 0.22 x 9.21 inches
Language: eng

Find more of our titles on our website. We have a selection of thousands of titles that will interest you. Please visit

www.triestepublishing.com